It's easy to entertain spiritual philosophy and vow to change in the midst of relative peace and plenty. Where the rubber meets the road is when life veers off course, and presents us with a significant personal challenge. This is, in two short sentences, why Shauna's story is so inspiring. I have taught many people how to apply the power of belief, but Shauna was special. Her physical difficulties are far beyond any I have known and yet she persisted, masterfully applying the power of belief to fulfill her greatest desires, despite the odds.

Ray Dodd, author, *The Power of Belief*

TO: Audrey,

You are a beautiful person & a gift & blessing in my life! I am so glad that our stress mastery journey brought you into my life! I am looking forward to staying in touch! :)
Thank you for everything!

Many Blessings to You!

Shauna Bruce - Hamburger
June 2019

BEYOND ADVERSITY

Into Freedom

by

Shauna Bruce-Hamburger

ACKNOWLEDGEMENTS

The experience of writing this book has stretched me and made me learn and grow beyond what I imagined. The completion of this book is truly a dream come true. I feel so very honored to have had this opportunity to share my story and wisdom with all of those who will read this book.

There are so many people who helped me with this book through their encouragement and belief in me. I owe my appreciation and gratitude to many people for helping make my book a reality.

First I would like to thank everyone at Insight Publishing for believing in me, for guiding me and supporting me along this journey. I am sincerely grateful for all of your encouragement, hard work, wisdom, and creative insight in putting this book together. I could not have completed this project without you. Thank you—each and every one of you!

I also want to thank my very dear friend Koree Khongphand-Buckman for helping me in such a tremendous way with the very meaningful project of the tribute to Shad's work in the audios in the back of this book. Your creative insight, hard work, wisdom, commitment, and perseverance with this project have meant more to me than you will ever know, as does your wonderful friendship. You are such an amazing and beautiful person, and I so appreciate you and your presence in me and my family's lives. We treasure you!

I also want to thank all of my wonderful family and friends who have supported, encouraged, and inspired me along this journey. I have such faithful family and friends who have believed in me all along the way and I can't thank all of you enough. For those of you who let me write about you and inspired me with your stories: I appreciate and thank you!

I thank my amazing family who has been supporting me in my dreams and goals ever since I was little. I thank you for being such a wonderful family and raising me with the faith and values that have helped me to get to where I am today. Thank you for the wonderful foundation you provided for me all of my life.

I thank my husband, Loren, for always believing in me and supporting me in this endeavor. To hear you tell me I have an important message to share has meant more to me than you will ever know! My husband, parents, and friends are all my rocks and I can't thank all of you enough.

Finally, and most importantly, I also want to thank the Lord Jesus; He is my everything!

DEDICATION

In honor of my late brother, Shad Ryon Bruce

(1976–2008):

Shad, you were always such an incredible inspiration of wisdom, courage, and selfless and unconditional love in the lives of those who were blessed enough to know you. I remember so many conversations with you about me getting my book written, and I wish you were here to see this project completed. However, I know you are cheering for me from Heaven.

It is my absolute honor to include you in this project, and to be able to share your amazing wisdom with the world. We always talked about doing a brother-sister project, and even though I would love to have done it with you here on this Earth, to be able to include you in my book means more than I can say.

Thank you, Shad, for being the truly wonderful and amazing brother and person that you were and for teaching all of us such powerful lessons about living a life that truly counts while you were here on this Earth. You made a beautiful mark on this world, Shad, and I am so very proud to be your sister! I love you! "See you at the top," Shad!

To my wonderful parents, Tom and Shari Bruce:

I can't thank you enough, Mom and Dad, for all of the life-changing wisdom that you taught me in my thirty-five years of living. I truly would not be the person I am today without both of you and all of your amazing wisdom. Your continued unconditional love, encouragement, and support of my dreams has meant more to me than you will ever know. I truly would not have been able to complete this project if it had not been for your support and wisdom about how to live a fulfilling and meaningful life.

Thank you for believing in me, Mom and Dad, and for encouraging me every step of the way. You have challenged me to live a higher level of living and I genuinely thank God for that and for you as my parents. I am a better person because of the wisdom you have taught me. You are both phenomenal examples of amazing human beings and I am so honored to call you my parents! I love you!

To my wonderful husband, Loren:

You are such a gift of God in my life! Your daily support, encouragement, and unconditional love for me this past year (our first year of marriage) has meant more to me than you will ever know. I truly find more reasons to love you every day. The laughter, wisdom, and encouragement you continually give me have meant more to me than I can even express. Thank you for believing in me and my message, honey. To have you appreciate and support the gifts God has put in me has been essential to my being able to complete this project.

You are a wonderful husband, Loren, and I am so thankful I have you by my side to walk through this life with. I love you, honey!

INTRODUCTION

I wrote this book in the hope that I can inspire and encourage you to discover and achieve your deepest level of joy, hope, and freedom, even in the midst of adverse and challenging circumstances that you may be facing.

As a Life Coach, Motivational Speaker, and a former massage therapist, I have met many people who are living a life of such struggle and imprisonment within adverse circumstances. As owner of my business "Divine Potential," I feel my greatest desire and most fulfilling purpose in life is to inspire and encourage people to live in their highest God-given potential and this book was born out of that desire.

In living with the permanent birth defect and disability of spina bifida for more than thirty-five years, I have discovered some foundational keys to living a life of true freedom and deep abiding joy, even in the midst of pain, loss, and hardship. The foundational truths shared in this chapter were written to help enable you to find the level of freedom you need so that you are no longer controlled by or imprisoned in your circumstances. This book is intended to help you master your life rather than living with your circumstances mastering you!

Although I live with the effects and physical issues of spina bifida every day, my physical challenges do not control, define, or limit me. That level of freedom and joy is my desire for all who read this book.

This book is not intended as a "just get over it" book. Although some of the keys in this book may at times seem challenging. To completely embrace them will require changes in your mental habits. They were meant to help you discover your greatest level of freedom and healing, even in the midst of your challenging circumstances.

In this book, I discuss part of the process of grief my family has experienced in losing my brother, Shad, in 2008. However, this book is not a book on grieving, so the process discussed in this book is not meant as a be-all, end-all journey in healing from grief. Healing from grief is a very individual journey, and I encourage you to seek out additional resources in your journey through this difficult healing process.

I absolutely believe what the Bible says in Ecclesiastes 3:1: "To everything there is a season, a time for every purpose under heaven." There is a time for everything in our lives, and I in no way want to take away from where you are in your journey. However, true transformation does require work and a willingness to let go of unhealthy habits and old ways of coping in order to embrace new ways of thinking and living.

If you find that you are living in challenging circumstances, if you feel lost and confined and feel you will never be able to move beyond "just getting through" your circumstances, then this book is for you. There is hope—you can get beyond "just struggling" in your circumstances and you can go beyond just getting back to square one. It is my hope that this book will help you find a whole new level of fulfillment, joy, hope, peace, and liberty, no matter what your circumstances are.

I pray, as the following quote says, that this book can help you find an entirely new life even in the midst of your adversity: "When you give someone a book, you don't give him just paper, ink, and glue. You give him the possibility of a whole new life"—Christopher Morley 1890–1957, novelist, journalist, and poet.

CHAPTER 1

THE POWER OF YOUR PERCEPTION

"It's not what you look at that matters, it's what you see"—Henry David Thoreau.

"You are free to choose, but the choices you make today will determine what you will have, be, and do in the tomorrow of your life" Zig Ziglar.

"God has given us two incredible things: absolutely awesome ability and freedom of choice. The tragedy is that, for the most part, many of us have refused them both" Frank Donnelly.

Webster's dictionary defines perspective as "The aspect in which a subject or its parts are mentally viewed." My favorite definition of perception is "The lens through which we look at (or see) our circumstances or life." Every day, all day, we as human beings are making decisions about our lives based on how we perceive life's situations. Understanding that we have the ability to choose our attitude, response, and perception is one of the greatest forms of empowerment in the midst of adverse circumstances. I believe that if you can change the way you view yourself and your life, you can completely change the quality of your life regardless of your current circumstances.

Due to having surgery on both of my feet when I was in kindergarten, I started school in a wheelchair. After going to school and realizing I was the only person in a wheelchair. I came home and asked my parents what was wrong with me and why was I in a wheelchair? My parents went on to explain to me that I was born with spina bifida. They explained to me what that was and how it was going to affect my life and me physically. It was in this conversation however that my parents gave me the most incredible and life changing wisdom that they would ever give me. My parents expressed to me that although I had spina bifida and I was going to have to live forever with the effects of it, I could either choose to live as a victim of spina bifida or I could choose to believe I was here for a reason that I had a purpose for my life and I could choose to live life to the fullest; despite having spina bifida.

I remember going in my room and telling God that day that I knew He made me for a reason and that I wanted to live life to the fullest, regardless of my physical circumstances. I learned that day that although I would always have circumstances in my life that I could not change or control, I could always choose my perception and attitude about those circumstances. I realized I was not powerless to my circumstances and I did not have to surrender to them and live a life controlled by my circumstances, because I could always choose my response to them.

It was through realizing that I had a choice in how I was going to live my life with spina bifida—that was the beginning of me living a life of freedom. In this chapter, I want to show you how your perception or view of your circumstances is a vital element in living your authentic life of wholeness, freedom, and abundant joy.

2

When my parents told me I could choose to live as a victim of spina bifida or not, they were basically telling me I had a choice about how I saw myself and therefore how I would live my life based on what I saw. The choice I made to live my life to the fullest was made because somehow, deep inside of me, I didn't see myself as a victim of spina bifida. If I had chosen to view myself as a victim, I would not be where I am today. The entire course of my life would have been very different just because of my perception being different.

To help you understand more of what my journey has been in life, I want to help you understand what spina bifida is and how it has affected me. Spina bifida means "open spine." It is the most common permanently disabling birth defect. It happens very early in the pregnancy. Some babies who have spina bifida are born with their spinal column not closed all of the way, and the nerves of the spine sometimes are protruding out from the opening in the spine.

There are three levels of spina bifida. I was born with the most severe form of spina bifida-myelomeningocele. I am in the very small percentage (5 percent) of people born with spina bifida who does not have a shunt in my head, as hydrocephalus (water on the brain) is also very common with spina bifida.

Because of the faith of my parents and the power of God, I know that several miracles have occurred in my life. When I was born, the doctors expressed to my parents that they did not know if I would live or, if I did live, if I would ever walk. My parents did the only thing they knew to do when they got that news—they went to the chapel in the hospital. At that time, I was having surgery to close my spine. I was four days old. My parents surrendered my life to God at that chapel in the hospital.

I did however start to develop hydrocephalus—my soft spot began bulging. The doctors expressed to my parents that if I did have to have a shunt that they actually can be pure hell. The doctors told my parents to take me home and bring me back in two weeks. The doctors expected me to have full-blown hydrocephalus by then. However, God had another plan. My mom who has always been such a strong woman

3

of faith, laid her hand on my bulging soft-spot and prayed every day during those two weeks. The excess fluid left and I did not need the dreaded shunt.

Because of the varying degrees of severity of spina bifida, it affects each child differently, but with the most severe form (the type I was born with) it usually causes severe permanent disabilities. These include varying degrees of nerve damage and loss of sensation and muscle and motor control in the feet, legs, bladder and bowels. My parents were told when I was an infant that had had my defect been only an inch higher on my back I would have been paralyzed. I can walk but I have a limp; and I wear a leg brace and an insert in my other shoe.

Shauna's older brother Shane and Shauna in her body cast at one year old.

The spina bifida also caused me to have dislocated hips, so when I was one year old, I was put in a body cast to try to correct that. My hip sockets did not completely form, so my hips just basically rest on the sockets; it is truly a miracle that I walk.

I had to wear many different splints, braces, and other casts on my legs throughout the first six years of my life to try to correct the deformities and loss of function due to permanent nerve damage. When I was six years old, I had my first surgery on my feet and legs—a tendon transplant.— I had another tendon transplant surgery on my right foot when I was ten and had part of my calcaneus bone removed, In fourth grade, I began wearing a brace on my left leg because I have "drop foot" and am not able to pick up my left foot to walk.

I also had nerve damage to my bladder, bowels, and kidneys, additional complications typical of spina bifida. I had my first bladder infection when I was two. I did have to endure a catheter while growing up because of the damage to my bladder and kidneys and I also have "reflux" in my kidneys which means my urine flows back up into my kidney instead of flowing out. While I was growing up, my

parents and I had to take great care to avoid kidney infections that could permanently damage my kidneys even further.

I was also told by a doctor, after he looked at an MRI of my brain, that my brain did not fully develop. He also said that other parts of my brain compensated for the undeveloped ones. Our bodies are such amazing creations!

Shauna in another brace to help with her dislocated hips.

I also discovered, about three years ago, that I have "tethered spine," which is also very common with spina bifida. It is a result of the scar tissue that develops around the incision site of the defect and causes more disabling affects, much like that already experienced with spina bifida, but worse. It also involves a lot of pain in the area of the tethering. I learned from a neurosurgeon three years ago that to have surgery on that area to free up the spine again could actually make me worse and make me lose more muscle control and feeling, so that is something that I also must deal with.

I am very fortunate because many children born with spina bifida endure many more surgeries than I have had to have. I have only had three—one to close my spine and two on my feet and legs.

My parents' perceptions of my abilities affected my life profoundly. The doctor who delivered me told my parents that the best advice he could give them in raising me would be for them to not treat me any differently than they did their other children. He told my parents that if their other children had chores, then I needed to have chores. If their other children were in extracurricular activities, I should also have extracurricular activities.

My parents spent their life raising me in the very same way they did my two brothers, and I am so very thankful for that. Had they treated me differently, I would have grown up being more "disabled" than I already was. I never would have become the independent person I am today.

A doctor once told me that I must have had tremendous parents in order for me to have graduated from college, have my own business, and to have been so active growing up. I was a cheerleader, in student council, I was junior class president, volleyball manager, and in 4-H. I competed very successfully on the speech team, among other things.

The doctor told me that he had seen some parents actually contribute to the problems of their special needs children more than the disability would have done because of the way they raised them. Some parents can be overprotective and some do not have high enough expectations. Because of the success that the doctor saw in me, he asked me to speak at a summer camp he held for special needs children. He wanted me to speak to the children and parents to help them understand how they could live successfully with a disability.

My parents always taught me that I could do whatever I put my mind to, therefore, I grew up knowing that deep down inside of me, whatever I wanted to do I could do . . . and I did.

I was also told by doctors that I would never be able to drive with my feet, but I taught myself how to, although I still mainly use hand controls.

I also wanted to be a massage therapist after graduating college. I earned my BS degree in Wellness Management but the college I wanted to attend to learn massage therapy would not accept me. They told me I could never be a massage therapist, yet I found a way and was a massage therapist for more than eight years.

Having my parents teach me that I could do whatever I put my mind to is what gave me the determination to not take no for an answer in life. I am very determined because my parents taught me to be.

My parents always kept me focused on what I could do rather than what I couldn't do, so I grew up being reminded of and focusing on what I was capable of and what my gifts and talents were rather than on what I couldn't do or wasn't good at. My parents were phenomenal at fostering my strengths and keeping me focused on what I could offer to the world rather than what I couldn't. They never let spina bifida define me or my life. Therefore, spina bifida is something I experience every single day, but it is not something that controls me or dictates who I am. Who I really am is who I am in my spirit and attitude.

I really do believe you live what you see when you look in the mirror. I believe that how you see yourself, your life, and your circumstances is what determines your behavior and actions. In my opinion, people's perceptions are what shapes their attitude and ultimately creates the environment in which they live. I know for certain that when I was growing up, if I had adopted the mindset that I was just a "crippled" or "disabled" person, I never would have done or become what I have done or am today. If I had adopted the mentality that I was a victim of a cruel disability, I never would have found freedom in the midst of those circumstances. It is my perception that has allowed me to find freedom in circumstances that I cannot control or change.

Victor Frankl, a holocaust survivor is someone I have been very inspired by. Victor spent more than three years in a concentration camp and also lost his entire family during that time.

It was in his book, *Man's search for Meaning,* that he discussed the ability to choose. He wrote, "Everything can be taken from a man but one thing: the last of the human freedoms—to choose one's attitude in any given set of circumstances, to choose one's own way." It was in Victor Frankl's understanding of his ability to choose that allowed him to live when many around him were perishing.

I also love the story that Oprah tells in her book, *What I Know for Sure.* In it she talks about how growing up in Mississippi, she would hear people all around her talking about the "dire circumstances for blacks." However, in her book, she tells how that picture or belief was not ever what she saw for herself. She wrote, "I believed I belonged to someone or something bigger than myself, my family, or even Mississippi. I believed I was God's child, therefore I could do anything." Now look at where Oprah is! Oprah's circumstances were the same as many people living in her time and location, however, what she saw about her life and her real potential changed the course of what could have been her life.

Where are you looking from?

When looking at your circumstances are you seeing them from a perspective that allows you to live your highest and most purposeful life? To find your greatest level of freedom in the midst of adversity, you have to move beyond "seeing" your life from your physical senses, and into seeing your life from the deepest place of truth inside of you—your spirit and the truth of God inside of you. Einstein said that you "can't solve a problem with the same mind that created it," so in order to live your true birthright of wholeness and freedom, you have to learn how to transcend your natural vision of what you see for your life. What you "see" with your natural senses can change in the blink of an eye, but what you know in your spirit to be true is where the real picture and vision for your life exists.

The Bible *(The Message* version) states in Matthew 6:22, "Your eyes are windows into your body. If you open your eyes wide in wonder and belief, your body fills up with light. If you live squinty-eyed in greed and distrust, your body is a dank cellar. If you pull the blinds on your windows, what a dark life you will have!" This passage paints a clear picture of the value of perspective and how the right perception of your life can change the course of your life.

Knowing you have the ability to choose your response and attitude and perception in life puts you in a position of being pro-active rather than reactive to life's circumstances. Proactive people don't let life's circumstances determine or dictate who and what they are or what they are going to be. Proactive people are not victims and take responsibility for their life regardless of how trying their circumstances are.

As I said earlier, we are all making choices every day based on what we "see" in our lives. So let me ask you this: what is it that you are really looking at in your life and how is that view affecting the quality of your life?

When I made the decision to live my life to my fullest potential rather than as a victim of spina bifida, I was going beyond my natural view of my life into what was inside of me—in my spirit. It would have been very easy at six years old to get stuck in the natural circumstances of braces, casts, wheelchairs, surgeries, walking with a limp, being "different," pain, rejection, and less than perfect health, but something inside of me caused me to see and choose from a higher place. Had I been lost in what I saw and felt in the natural and aligned myself with those feelings, I never would have lived the quality of life that I am right now.

What is in the natural is not our highest place of truth unless we allow it to be. It all is just a reflection of our perception—what we are looking at and where we are looking from!

9

Ask yourself right now if you are living your life from your highest place of truth—from a picture of unlimited potential—or are the pictures you hold in your mind keeping you from reaching your highest potential? I think we all were created with unlimited potential, but the pictures we have in our minds, our beliefs about ourselves, and our limited perceptions can limit who we become!

What do you see?

I don't think it is too strong of a statement to say that the quality of life you are living is a direct reflection of how you see yourself and your circumstances. Your view of you is the life of you! If my only view of me was a person living with spina bifida, my life would be all about spina bifida. Living with spina bifida does not change or dictate the quality of my life neither does it dictate how I see myself. I am reminded of this when those closest to me tell me that when they look at me they don't even see spina bifida. I believe that is because I, too, don't see the spina bifida! Has this always come easy for me? No. I would be lying to you if I told you that every day I don't see spina bifida, but even through the circumstances that have been the most painful in living with spina bifida, I know that I always have a choice in how I am going to view those circumstances and I always have a choice in what I give my thoughts and power too. I have heard it said that your perception is more powerful than your reality, which to me is so true because it is your perception that becomes your reality

How you see yourself, your life, and your circumstances directly determines your behavior and actions. It is my perception that has allowed me to find freedom in circumstances that I cannot control or change

Earl Nightingale said "We can let circumstances rule us, or we can take charge and rule our lives from within." When we can look at things from the perspective of our spirit and attitude, and remember that we always have the ability to choose; I believe we will see we are already whole, and that is where we will find our freedom. But when we look outside ourselves (at our circumstances) for who we are, we will never find the truth of whom we really are, that will come only from looking within.

I truly believe we were all created by God to flourish and thrive, yet so many times we become so stuck in our circumstances that we don't live up to our highest potential. We let our circumstances create a life of settling for much less than we deserve or were created for.

Realizing your ability to choose your response, attitude, and perception in every situation can truly move you out of a place of mediocrity and "just existing" into greatness. Our ability to choose is one of the greatest God-given gifts we have, yet so many times we throw that gift away and settle for so much less in life.

We don't always get to choose our circumstances, but the one thing no person or situation can ever take away from us is our ability to choose how we react to them. That ability is something God gave all of us. Free will is the ability to make choices in life and that can never be taken away, no matter what our circumstances are.

I love and will end with this quote by William James. "The greatest revolution of our generation is the discovery that human beings, by changing the inner attitudes of their minds, can change the outer aspects of their lives."

Questions for the Reader:

How would your quality of life change if you chose to see the trying circumstances in your life differently?

How could you begin today to look at your circumstances through a different "lens" in order to enable you to live a richer more rewarding life?

CHAPTER 2

THE POWER OF GRATITUDE

"Of all the 'attitudes' we can acquire, surely the attitude of gratitude is the most important and by far the most life-changing"— Zig Ziglar.

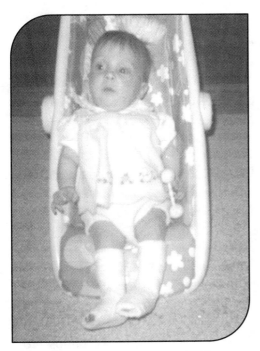

Shauna in her first casts at 10 weeks old.

From the time I was old enough to remember, my parents taught me how to be thankful for what I have in life and for what my abilities were rather than focusing on what I didn't have or on what my "disability" was. I am very grateful that my parents were wise enough to help me understand that I would get much further in life if I would stay focused on the gifts and blessings I had been given, rather than focusing on what I couldn't do or on what was "wrong" with my body.

My parents helped me understand at a very early age, that although I did have many major issues in my body to deal with on a daily basis, and would have to deal with for the rest of my life, things could always be worse. I do believe that no matter how bad things seem to be in our lives, things could always be worse and we can always find someone who is worse off than we are. I know we have all read the Persian Proverb: "I cried because I had no shoes, until I saw someone who had no feet."

I heard it said once: "self-pity is a useless emotion—nothing good comes from it." I absolutely agree with this statement. Many times I could have chosen the attitude of self-pity, but had I chosen self-pity rather than gratitude, I would not be where I am today, neither would I have the quality of life that I do. I truly believe that what you think about most expands, and when we focus on what we are grateful for and on the goodness in our lives, we create more things to be thankful for.

Gratitude is an empowering attitude. When we choose to be grateful for what we have right now in this moment, it removes us from the state of living as a powerless victim. When we are going through adversity or challenging circumstances, it is so easy to get lost in the thoughts of anger, disappointment, self-pity, and depression and focus on what we have lost, rather than on what we still have.

Adversity is almost always the loss of something, whether it be the loss of a job, your health, or a loved one, yet even in the midst of those losses, we always still have things to be thankful for. Remembering the things we have is what keeps us moving forward in life, rather than stopping or getting stuck in the midst of our challenges.

Being grateful for what we still have helps us remember what is truly important in life such as the irreplaceable treasures of our family and friends. In her book, *The Right Questions,* Debbie Ford wrote, "When we are looking for what's right, we invite life to shower us with all of its many gifts. When we look for what's wrong, we choose to view ourselves through the narrowest possible lens."

When we choose to not be grateful for what we still have in life, even in the midst of loss, we lose so much more. We lose sight of what really matters in life and what we still have to offer, and we end up taking so much for granted.

In July 2008, my family and I experienced the greatest loss any of us had ever faced. My thirty-two-year-old brother, Shad, suddenly and unexpectedly passed away! My brother was a wonderful, amazing man who was so full of life and love for everyone he met. He was in the midst of becoming a motivational speaker and wanted to spend his life helping people.

A year and a half before his passing, my brother was in a tragic motorcycle accident. He suffered a very serious head injury that eventually led to his death. In the midst of losing my brother, my family and I had many moments when we wondered how we would ever go on. We wondered how we could ever possibly move past the pain of losing someone so young who was so full of life unlived and someone we all loved so very much.

In the midst of our darkest hours of our unbelievable pain and grief, my family and I held on to all that we had left—the power of God and all that we had to be thankful for in this situation, which was a lot, even in the midst of losing one of the most wonderful people we all had ever known.

Immediately, in the midst of the loss of my brother, my family and I began to think of all of the things we still had to be grateful for in that circumstance. Things could have ended for my brother in a much more tragic way due to his head injury, and it was hanging on to the blessings we could see that helped us move forward.

In the midst of those blessings, we could still see the goodness of God, we could still see His hand of protection, and we could still see the favor of God for my brother. One of the blessings we were most thankful for is that when my brother passed away, he was in love with and greatly loved by a beautiful, amazing woman whom he was going to marry. We still to this day are thankful for the love my brother knew with the love of his life, Autumn. (Autumn also has a precious daughter, Skye, whom Shad also loved dearly.) However, if as a family we had not held on to what we still had to be thankful for in the midst of that tragedy, I don't know how much our healing would have been hindered. We could have chosen to be bitter or angry because the motorcycle accident was not my brother's fault. Although he was not wearing a helmet, it was the driver of another vehicle who did not see my brother at an intersection and hit him. However, what good would it have done for us to be bitter or angry? It would only have greatly hindered our healing and our future.

Because my brother wanted to be a motivational speaker, and was not able to make his work available before he passed away, I included some of his best motivational audios on the CD in the back of this book.

I love the quote from Myla Kabat-Zinn, "Each difficult moment has the potential to open my eyes and open my heart." I believe this is so because each difficult moment in life causes us to look deeper at the true treasures in our lives and causes us to really embrace all that is truly valuable. Each difficult moment also causes us to find the deeper meaning of life.

Gratitude truly is a powerful healer and motivator. In his book, *Let Go of Whatever Makes You Stop,* John L Mason wrote, "Thanksgiving, you will find, will create power in your life because it opens the generators of your heart to respond gratefully, to receive joyfully, and to react creatively." I believe the keys to freedom in the midst of adversity are whatever keeps you moving forward, and gratitude does that!

An attitude of gratitude changes the way we see things. However an attitude of gratitude is a *choice*. When we are going through difficulties in life, we can feel as though we have no choice in how or what we think, but the good news is that we do! In difficult times, we have to assert real effort in preventing our minds from wandering and dwelling on the hardships and difficulties of our lives. We have to continue to nourish our faith, inner strength, and a vision for our future. Gratitude is a choice because we do get to choose daily what we are going to focus on and when we choose to focus on the good in our lives, we naturally develop an attitude of gratitude.

One of the most powerful stories I remember about someone choosing an attitude of gratitude was when I was doing some coaching with Ray Dodd, author of *The Power of Belief* and founder of Powerofbelief.com.

Ray was in a very serious skiing accident during the time I was a client of his. The skiing accident was not in any way Ray's fault, and the person who hit him on the ski slopes, never looked back to see if Ray was okay. Ray was not okay. After the impact, Ray was seriously injured and had to spend some time in the hospital because of damage to his lungs.

After Ray was released from the hospital and returned to our coaching sessions, I asked him more about the accident. He told me that the only thing he was telling people when they asked about the incident, were all of the things that had been good about it and the things he was grateful for that involved the situation. He told me about how wonderful the nurses and doctors were, how supported he had been, how quickly he was healing, and how grateful he was for all of the positive things in that circumstance.

When I told him how amazed I was at his incredible response, he asked me, "Shauna, what good would it do for me to rehearse how bad

17

the situation was and the negativity of the situation? What would that do?"

"It would only hinder your healing process," I replied.

"Shauna you are exactly right!" he agreed.

Ray could have chosen to tell his story from the viewpoint of a victim. Yes, he truly was ruthlessly injured by another person, but Ray knew the power of the stories we tell ourselves in our circumstances and the power of gratitude and how being grateful is truly the key to healing properly in mind, spirit, and body.

Ray knew the power of gratitude in helping to heal his injured body; however, that concept is something most of us are not even aware of. In doing research for this book, I found so many intriguing studies on the power of gratitude and the affect it has on our mental, emotional, spiritual, and physical health.

I have always known that gratitude plays a significant role in a person's sense of well-being. However, it has been proven that those who keep gratitude journals have higher levels of reported alertness, enthusiasm, determination, optimism, and energy. They also experience less depression and stress, and they sleep better and exercise more.

What intrigued me most in doing my research were the findings and thoughts of Phillip Watkins, an East Washington University Psychologist. In the article it discussed Watkins' experiments, which have shown that, "Traumatic memories fade into the background for people who regularly feel grateful, and troublesome thoughts pop up less frequently and with less intensity." The article also discussed Watkins' suggestions that "gratitude may enhance emotional healing." His experiments also showed that "thankfulness helps the brain more fully process events, and grateful people achieve closure by making sense of negative events, so that they can come to a more positive outlook." (*Psychology Today,* "Make a Gratitude Adjustment," by Lauren Aaronson, March 1, 2006.)

I think these findings are truly incredible! This power to bring healing to our own hearts and minds is something that is within our reach every single day. It is so very simple, yet it can seem elusive.

We all have heard the saying, "Pain is inevitable but suffering is optional." We all are going to encounter painful or adverse circumstances in our lives, but it is how we choose to see and respond to those circumstances that will determine the course of our lives. I absolutely believe that choosing your attitude in life determines your direction and your destiny.

Life is full of opportunities for giving thanks, yet there is a difference between experiencing and expressing grateful moments and having a grateful attitude. I believe gratitude is a matter of habit, but it is also a state of mind. A grateful attitude changes the way we see things, which changes the way we respond to life. An attitude of gratitude takes us out of the victim mentality and puts us into the place of strength and empowerment because we choose to see all of the blessings and gifts we have been given. When we see life from a more positive vantage point, we are more likely to respond in a productive way. Gratitude is also infectious; it raises the emotional level of all of those around us, which improves life for everyone we come into contact with.

In my vocation as a motivational speaker, I almost always discuss the importance of an attitude of gratitude in all of my seminars and keynotes. One year, I was speaking at a national conference for people with disabilities. I discussed the importance of an attitude of gratitude and my gratefulness each and every day that although I walk with a limp and a brace, and have many other health issues, I can still walk. Many people born with spina bifida do not walk. As I was expressing my gratitude for being able to walk, an attendee who was in a wheelchair asked me, "But what about those of us who don't walk? What do we have to be grateful for?"

My heart broke for this girl as she asked her question. Yes, this precious girl is in a wheelchair, a hardship I cannot even imagine. What I expressed to this girl was that although she is in a wheelchair, she still has gifts, talents, and abilities she can choose to be thankful for every day. I went on to tell her that she still has a mind that works, she still has eyes that work, hands that work, a mouth, nose, and ears that work, and she still has a purpose for her life and gifts that the world around her needs. Though living in a wheelchair, she has things to offer this world that only she can give, in the way she can give them.

What saddened me greatly for that precious girl was that she only saw how hard her struggles are in a wheelchair. She had given away so much that she still had to offer and to be thankful for, all because she could not see it! This beautiful girl is so much more than just a girl in a wheelchair, just as I am so much more than a woman who lives with spina bifida, yet if I let that define me, rather than recognizing the gifts I still have, my gifts, talents, and abilities would all be wasted because I could not see past my challenging circumstances.

When we let our problems or circumstances define us or tell us who we are and where we will go in life, we surrender our power and end up living far below our true God-given potential. I choose to see hardships as something to make me grow and become wiser, better, and stronger. If we will let them, our tragedies can become our greatest steppingstones. Whenever we choose to focus on the hardships or adversities of our lives, and only see those, we lose sight of so much more.

Mac Anderson, founder of "Successories" said, "If we face our problems and respond to them positively, refusing to surrender to panic, bitterness, or self-pity, the adversities that come along to bury us, usually possess the potential to benefit us."

My own attitude of gratitude goes much deeper than just the way I think; it also is a result of my deep spiritual connection. One of my favorite scriptures in the Bible is, "Give thanks continually in all things"—Ephesians 5:20. My spiritual connection to God is a large part of why and how I am able to be grateful every day in the midst of continual challenges. I know deep down that God made me for a purpose and my life matters. That is why I can be thankful even when life hurts—no matter what I go through, there is a reason I am here and I have things I must do on this Earth. In that light, so many other things in life look small. I do feel that it is important that we be aggressively thankful. I also feel that this is what the above scripture is saying.

So how does one go about forming the principles of gratitude in one's life? As I said earlier, gratitude is a state of mind as well as a habit. To create the habit of gratitude, it is vital for us to acknowledge our blessings regularly! I have learned to focus on what I am grateful for so much that throughout the days of my life, I will be thanking God for what my husband and I have—good health, good job, a warm, wonderful home, running vehicles, and loving family and friends.

There are many ways we can begin to practice gratitude. I personally believe that we should not let one day pass without a few moments spent in giving thanks for our blessings. So, how do we go about starting to practice this if we have never done so before?

One of the easiest ways to begin practicing gratitude is every night before you go to bed, make a mental or actual list of the three to five things you are most grateful for that day. In your list-making, I challenge you to not just write down or make a mental note of the "easy" things you have to be grateful for. Writing down your dog, cat, and home might be easy, but to really learn to develop an attitude of gratitude, I encourage you to dig deeper inside of yourself. Really think about the blessings in your life and what you are most thankful for. Challenge yourself to consider such things as your best character traits, your greatest talents, or your most wonderful childhood moments and the virtues they taught you. It is also important that you record the simple things in your life such as the feel of the warm sun on your face and hot running water in your home. An attitude of gratitude can be so very simple, yet when you really dig deep to honor the things you have to be thankful for—things that you have never given any credence to before—then it really becomes life-changing.

21

Gratitude lists are a wonderful way to get started on your journey of gratefulness, but some people prefer to use "gratitude journals." You can use these in any manner you choose. Some people record things they are grateful for every day in a list format. I know of other people who write about the experiences and blessings of the day that they are most grateful for. Many people use gratitude journals and keep them for years so that they can look back at them when they choose, just to remember all of the good fortune they have had in their lives.

When my brother passed away, my mom heard of an idea on the *Good Morning America* television show. It was for those who were experiencing hardship or tragedy. The idea was to keep a "Blessings Journal." The idea of this is a little different than a gratitude journal. The "blessings journal" is used to record the various blessings of the days and weeks of one's life as one is in the midst of a trying circumstance. In essence, it is a recording of the things that are going right in the midst of things that may be very hard.

On the first Christmas after my brother passed away, his high school love and girlfriend, Koree, who is still a wonderful gift to my family's lives (and was such a help in getting Shad's audios ready for the back of this book), gave my family and me journals as Christmas presents. My mom and I were so thankful for the new journals and since we had heard of the idea of the "blessings journal" that is when we decided to use her gifts as our "blessings journals." So, in the midst of healing from the loss of my brother, we recorded and were so thankful for the blessings that we could still see occurring every day, even in the midst of our heartache. I still have and use that blessings journal. It has been a tremendous gift to read about all I have continually been blessed with in my life, even in those times when I have hurt the most.

I also feel it is imperative that we learn to show our gratitude in word and deed! In order for people to receive our appreciation, we have to first express it. I once heard a Pastor say, "Love not expressed is love not received." I think it is the same with gratitude. Too often it seems much easier to say "Thank You" to an acquaintance rather than to those who mean the most to us.

When I was growing up, it was a rule in our home to write thank you cards to those who did something or gave us something for which we were grateful. But today I think that is a lost art in our "instant" society, and yet it takes so very little time to sit down and write a thank you note or to show people how much you really appreciate them.

Another idea is an actual letter of gratitude maybe to someone who did something wonderful for you when you were a child whom you never expressed your gratitude to, or to someone you really appreciate in your life right now.

The last Christmas I ever saw my late brother, Shad, was the Christmas of 2007. That year, as gifts to my family members, I decided to write letters to each, telling them how much I loved them and exactly why I appreciated them. My letters that year were the hit of Christmas. They brought many hugs and heartfelt tears of gratitude.

It was July of 2008 when my brother passed away and I had not seen him since that Christmas of 2007. As we reached my brother's home in Florida to take care of his arrangements, the letter I wrote him that Christmas before was hanging on his refrigerator—almost eight months after he had received it! I can't tell you how very elated I was to see that letter because then I knew how very much it meant to him.

Unfortunately, we never know when it might be our last time to express to our loved ones how much we love and appreciate them! I will never have one regret. I will never have to wonder if my brother knew how amazing he was or how much I loved and appreciated him, because I took the time to tell him and I am so very thankful that I did!

It is my hope that through this chapter, you can see how the power of a grateful mindset can help you heal from the hardships you may be enduring in your life, as well as be a vital motivator to keep you moving forward so that you can get on to the business of living and

23

embracing life, even if you are facing circumstances that are hard and painful. I know from personal experience that no matter how painful or hard life may be, there are always still things to be thankful for. Embracing and recognizing those things and developing an attitude of gratitude will take you much further than you ever dreamed you could go!

I will even take it a step further—I predict that as you begin to develop a thankful heart and mindset of gratitude for all of the blessings you have been given, even in the midst of adversity, you eventually will even find yourself being thankful for the challenges you may be going through. At that point, you will have become not just someone with a grateful attitude, but you will have then become a grateful "person."

Questions for the Reader:

What is the one thing you can and will do today to begin to create the habit and an attitude of gratitude?

Are there any trying circumstances or tragedies in your life right now that you would be able to heal from or move forward in if you could recognize and acknowledge what you still have to be grateful for? If so, how can you begin to be more grateful in these experiences? What blessings can you see in the midst of this tragedy? Hang onto those blessings, because they are what will pull you through this trying time.

CHAPTER 3

CHANGE THE WAY YOU TALK, CHANGE YOUR LIFE

"Watch your thoughts, they become words. Watch your words, they become actions. Watch your actions, they become habits. Watch your habits, they become your character. Watch your character; it becomes your destiny"—Frank Outlaw.

Did you know that the most powerful words in the English language are the words you choose to say to yourself? The words we choose to say hold extraordinary power in our lives. They are what determine our direction, and are at the core of our success or defeat. Self-talk is the endless stream of thoughts that run through our heads every day. Some of these thoughts come from our own reason and logic and others come from interpretations or misconceptions we create about the events in our lives. Our self-talk or internal dialogue is something we usually are not even aware of; however, it has profound effects on our daily lives as well as our abilities and potential.

Even though it is not out loud, and we usually aren't aware of it, we talk to ourselves all of the time through our thoughts, internal questions, and beliefs. Unfortunately, most of the time our self-talk is negative, especially when we are in the midst of hardships or facing our darkest hours. The Minirth-Meier Series of "Worry-Free Living" states that we carry on internal conversations with ourselves "at a phenomenal rate of some thirteen hundred words per minute." However, we are usually not even aware of this non-stop flow of internal communication.

Would you like to become more aware of your internal dialogue, and better understand this concept of your own self-talk? If you said yes, I would like to suggest the following exercise.

To start, you will need to set a timer for twenty minutes throughout several hours of a day or period of days. When the timer goes off each twenty minutes, stop what you were doing and tune into what you were just saying to yourself. What conversation were you having in your head? Was it positive or negative? I think you might be amazed to discover how much negative self-talk is going on inside your head most of the time. I consider myself a very optimistic person, and when I did this exercise myself for the first time, I truly was shocked to discover how often I was carrying on a negative conversation in my head. I was thinking thoughts I was not even aware of having!

Unfortunately, when we are facing challenges in life, we can easily find ourselves saying negative things about ourselves and our circumstances. Some of the things we say are: "I am just too—old, young, tired, sick, stupid, broke, fat, tall, short, etc." "I will never be able to—lose this weight, find another job, find love again, etc." "I am never going to get that promotion," "We will never—" "I can't—because—" "I'm not—"

Do any of these phrases sound familiar? Have you said any of these words to yourself in the last week? Unfortunately, when we use these types of words, we essentially are giving our power away to our circumstances and letting them control us rather than empowering ourselves to be able to overcome our circumstances. Speaking these types of words will only create more defeat in your life and imprison you, which will never help you move forward into the life you really want. Negative self-talk can actually lead to depression and despair and create anger, as well as feed our frustrations! On the other hand, positive self-talk enables us to handle life in a more productive way. Our internal words, thoughts, and beliefs are the most essential keys to changing our lives and causing us to be who we want to be.

Did you know that whatever you say out loud often enough, your mind eventually believes, and what your mind believes filters into your subconscious and constantly gets replayed? Your subconscious mind only believes what you tell it, and it doesn't know the difference between the real or the imagined. Our minds can be compared to a computer and what you put into it gets stored and affects what comes out. So it is imperative that we fill our minds with positive input every day, especially when we are facing difficulties.

If we want to change the circumstances in our lives, and go beyond our adversity, we must change our thoughts as we have been discussing in earlier chapters, but we must also change the way we talk. As I said earlier, words truly are one of the most powerful things on the planet as far as what you do and where you go in your life. The old saying from our childhood of "sticks and stones will break my bones, but words will never hurt me," simply is not true. Our words can and do hurt us. In fact, our words can destroy our future and our potential or they can increase our motivation, improve our state of mind, help us find solutions, and lead to other positive changes in our behavior. It all depends on that internal conversation inside all of us and if it is positive or negative. The words we use in describing our lives are the seeds we are planting into the soil of our lives.

Although I didn't comprehend it then, the impact of my own internal dialogue affected me early in my life. Because my parents always taught me that "I could do whatever I put my mind too," I believed that to be true. Whenever I would face challenges or difficulties in life, I would always hear my parents' voices telling me "I could do whatever I put my mind too" and those words were what took me to where I am today.

Whenever I faced circumstances when people would tell me I could not or would not be able to do things that I wanted to do in life, I automatically internally refuted their "no's" because of what my parents and I had been saying all of my life—I can do whatever I put my mind to!

Therefore, I have taught myself how to drive with my feet, when doctors said it would never be possible; I walk, when doctors didn't think it would be possible; I became a very successful massage therapist was and continued in that profession for more than eight years, even though a massage therapy school told me I could not do it. I even was a cheerleader in middle school for two years, and competed in a race at a fourth grade track day while on crutches and with a cast on my foot. And all because of my internal voice that always told me I could do whatever I put my mind too. So because of my internal dialogue of "I can," I have never taken someone else's "no" or "you can't" as an answer to what was possible in my life.

If we want to transform our lives, it is critical that we truly understand the impact our words have. Our words can limit our potential, keep us "stuck" in our circumstances, or transform our lives for the better. Habitual negative self-talk creates limiting beliefs, which can hold us back for years until we become aware of it and work to change it. This is because the words we speak really become labels that we are putting on ourselves or our situations. Positive self-talk can truly help us find new levels of freedom in our situations.

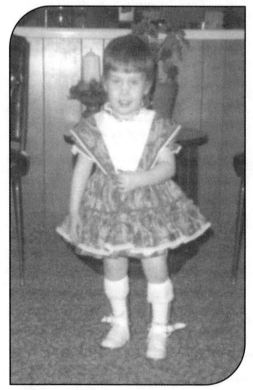

Shauna at two and a half years old in her first braces.

If, when growing up, I had never heard and believed the words of "I could do whatever I put my mind to," I am certain I would not be where I am today. Because our subconscious mind tends to believe the thoughts it hears, had I heard a different or

30

more negative message growing up rather than the encouraging, positive message that I did, I am certain my life would have turned out very differently. Because my parents never spoke to me about or brought attention to my "limitations," I was never aware of "limitations" or things that I couldn't do in my life.

The messages we hear in our lives and the messages we tell ourselves truly do have the ability to limit and imprison us, and that is because our self-talk tends to become a self-fulfilling prophecy. Our own words and the words of others really do color our experiences and also determine our perceptions of ourselves and others.

For example, if you are in the dentist's chair and he or she tells you, "This is really going to hurt a lot," or "you will experience some mild discomfort," no matter what the procedure is, you will tend to experience what the dentist told you that you would.

I love a story I have read about Muhammad Ali. He knew how to use the power of the spoken word to his mental and physical advantage. Even when Mohammad was known as a struggling fighter, he repeatedly declared himself "The Greatest." Ali believed in himself and he spoke those words out loud and often. Ali's now famous words of "I am the greatest" have made headlines around the world. Ali's inner belief, reflected outwardly, proved his beliefs to be true! What I think is interesting, is that Ali did not tell the world he was "probably" or "maybe" or "almost the greatest" he told himself and the world that he was "the greatest" and because of that inner conviction, now he is known all over the world as "The Greatest."

To prove to you the impact your own words have on your life and how something as simple as the example above really could have such a large effect, I want you to try another exercise with me. This exercise is simply to help you see the difference of how negative or positive statements can truly impact us. This is an exercise I teach in my "Stress-Less and Be More Productive" seminar to demonstrate the power of our self-talk.

To begin, I want you to say out loud a long, negative statement about yourself (remember, this is only an exercise). Then I want you to close your eyes and think about what you are feeling in your mind, emotions, and body. What do you feel? Can you describe it? Did you feel negative responses inside after saying that negative statement? Most people do. In fact, when doing this exercise at my seminars, I have had many people say things such as they felt like they had the flu or other unpleasant experiences.

Now, we are going to do the opposite; I want you to say out loud a long, positive statement about yourself. Then I want you to again close your eyes and think about what you are feeling in your mind, emotions, and body. How do you feel now? Is what you are experiencing positive? Most people experience very positive reactions when they say the positive statement. Usually, after the positive phrase is stated, the room is full of smiling people as I ask them to close their eyes and think about what they are feeling. Literally most of the room is smiling because of how wonderful that one positive statement made them feel.

Doing this exercise at my seminars is fun for me because it is so enlightening for my participants to realize how much affect their very own words have on their emotions, mental state, and physical health. In fact, much research throughout the years has shown the impact our mental state has on our health. Research has shown many health benefits that positive thinking may provide. Some of these benefits include increased life span, lower rates of depression, decreased levels of distress, increased resistance to the common cold, better psychological and physical well-being, decreased risk of death from cardiovascular disease, as well as better coping skills.

So where does our self-talk come from? I have heard it said that our "words are the clothes our thoughts wear." Matthew 12:34 says, "Out of the abundance of the heart, the mouth speaks." Our thoughts really do create the words we speak, so becoming more aware of the thoughts we think and replacing those negative thoughts with positive ones is of utmost importance. As the quote at the beginning of the chapter states, our thoughts turn into the words we speak.

Understanding that is essential in transforming your adverse circumstances. When our thoughts are positive, ambitious, grateful, encouraging, supportive, hopeful, and expectant of the best in life, our words will be as well!

Even the Apostle Paul tells us in the Bible how we can transform our lives by controlling our self-talk. He tells us in Philippians 4:8 what to concentrate on and think about: "Finally, brethren, whatsoever things are true, whatsoever things are honorable, whatsoever things are just, whatsoever things are pure, whatsoever things are lovely, whatsoever things are of good report; if there be any virtue, and if there be any praise, think on these things." The Bible is full of wisdom and scriptures concerning our words. One of my favorite scriptures is Matthew 21:21: "If you say to this mountain 'Be removed and be cast into the sea,' it will be done." This scripture clearly demonstrates to us the power of our words. I do believe we can speak positively to and about the negative circumstances in our lives and then see them changed!

I also truly love the following scriptures when considering the power our words have. Proverbs 18:21 states: "Death and Life are in the power of the tongue." And Proverbs 16:24 says: "Pleasant words are like a honeycomb, sweetness to the soul and health to the bones." These scriptures state that our words carry the power of life and death and even bring health to our bodies! These scriptures clearly show the incredible impact that our words have on our lives and our health as well as the lives of those who hear our words!

Before we begin to discuss solutions to our self-talk sabotages, I want to be sure you understand the importance of your self-talk and its impact on your life. I want to make this concept real for you. It is essential that you are able to identify how your negative self-talk has been wrong or erroneous.

What has been false about what you have been saying to yourself concerning your most adverse circumstances? To identify that, I want you to write down all the negative things you have said to yourself

33

lately about your most challenging circumstances. As you look at these statements, I want you to identify what you have been saying to yourself that is not true. An example of this could be, "I will never be able to lose this weight." That statement simply is not true. I truly believe we have been given everything we need in life to cause us to succeed and to reach our goals and live our dreams. The only thing that gets in the way is our beliefs about ourselves and our abilities.

The next step in this identification process is to then think about what behavior this erroneous self-talk has created. Ask yourself, "How has this erroneous self-talk hindered me from reaching my goals? What have my false statements made me believe that have actually created self-defeating behavior?"

Then, after identifying what is false about the messages you have been telling yourself and how those messages have been affecting your behavior, I want you to write down an alternative statement that is true or accurate about your situation. What is good about yourself in this circumstance? An example of this for the above negative statement would be, "I am able to accomplish my health goals." As Dr. Phil always says, "We cannot change what we don't acknowledge." Identifying how false your negative self-talk really has been, and identifying how those false statements have negatively influenced your behavior, and turning the false into the positive truth, can and will drastically transform your life. I have seen this concept many times in my life and in my clients' lives.

I remember a very simple example of how the above concept affected me in my own life. In June of 2009, all in one week's time, I was getting married in one state, packing up my apartment, and moving to another state. I literally was moving from one to another state and getting married in another state, all within one week's time! Needless to say I was very stressed and overwhelmed. As I let my thoughts of stress get to me, my words became very negative about the situation. I kept saying to my family and friends, "I can't do this." "This is too hard." "This is too much to do in only one week." As I kept saying these statements to my family and friends, my mom finally

34

said to me, "Shauna, do you know how many negative statements you have made about your situation?" And she was right—I had been only speaking negatively about the situation. And guess what? The more I said, "I just can't do this, this is too much," the more I felt like I could not do it. I lost physical energy, I allowed my feelings of being overwhelmed to control me, and it was only getting harder to do anything. My mom helped me recognize how negative I was being, although I realized I should not be making such negative statements. After my mom helped bring my self-talk to my attention, I started saying to myself, "I can do this. This is not too hard and I will get everything done that I need to do." Changing my language literally changed my behavior, and when I got my speaking on track, I got the outcome I wanted—I did get everything done and got married and moved all in less than one week!

So, where do we begin when trying to transform our self-talk into more positive, life-affirming words? My favorite technique is the use of daily affirmations. A positive affirmation is a positive, proactive, present tense statement that begins with "I am" and ends with a positive character trait, attitude, behavior, or attribute.

Remember the list of negative statements we discussed at the beginning of the chapter? All of those negative statements began with "I will never" "I can't" "I won't" I'm not." Aren't these the typical statements we use when life gets hard? Well, now we are going to work on changing those statements into positive statements. When you use positive affirmations, you want to use statements that describe your situations the way you desire them to be.

Examples of some positive affirmations are:

- I am a beautiful and loving person

- I am fully capable of achieving my goals

- I am strong and well-educated

- I am hopeful about my future

- I am capable of living a healthy, fulfilling life

When you make these types of statements, you are choosing to honor and affirm your own life and the value and strengths of your life. As you think about your most challenging circumstances in your life right now, or the area of your life where you have felt the most negativity, make a list of a few positive affirmations about that situation(s) and put them on three-inch by five-inch cards; take them with you wherever you go. Then, whenever you start to feel yourself thinking or speaking negatively about your circumstances, read your positive affirmations. This will help you get back on the track of affirming your life, rather than destroying it with your words. Your positive affirmations will not only increase your confidence and peace, but they will also bolster your self-esteem and move you more toward the life you desire.

Another key method to changing your negative self-talk is replacing your negative statements immediately with accurate positive ones. This method is not denial—life can be very painful and challenging at times, and it is never good to live in denial—but when our words are negative, we tend to stop looking for answers to our problems or trials, which only hinders us more. So immediately changing negative statements into true and positive statements, and believing what you say, is key to keep you moving forward.

An example is instead of saying, "This is going to be a terrible day," you could immediately replace that comment with the positive statement of, "I am grateful for this day and grateful to be alive. This is going to be a beautiful day!" Can you feel the difference in the two statements and how they make you feel just saying them? Don't you think the positive statement is going to get you further than the negative one?

Another solution is one I love to challenge myself to do now and then—I go on a "complaint fast." I challenge myself to do this when I experience negative situations such as sickness. It is so easy to complain when we don't feel good; doing that only makes us feel worse.

This month, as I am writing this book, I have been sick the entire month and it has been very challenging for me not to complain about how bad I feel or how tired I am of being sick. When I would complain, I would only feel worse. Not only does our mind believe what we say, but so does our body! When I told my husband that I was only going to proclaim good things about my health and my body, I started feeling much better. Even when I was not feeling my best and people would ask how I was feeling I would only allow myself to say positive statements about how I was doing. I never lied and I was not in denial, I just wasn't voicing or focusing on how bad I felt.

When you do a complaint fast, you make a commitment to not complain about anything to anybody for a specific period of time; it can be for however long you want it to be. It is best if you can go on this fast with a family member or friend to help keep you accountable. The goal here is not perfection, but rather to become more aware of how often you complain and how complaining is making you feel. Eventually you will find yourself focusing more on the positive things in your life, which will leave you feeling more grateful, happy, and content.

If you are a chronic complainer, and have created a habit of speaking more about the negative, you can try doing the complaint fast for twenty-one days. It takes twenty-one days to form or break a habit. Choose for the next twenty-one days to only engage in positive self-talk. When you find yourself saying something negative, simply change it to something positive. You really will find, as you continue this exercise, that your negative thoughts have been replaced with much more positive thoughts, which will transform your quality of life. This exercise truly will help you get out of your rut, as speaking habits can be changed.

In closing, I am reminded of the story of a young woman who came up to talk to me after one of my seminars. In the seminar, I talked about the importance and impact of positive self-talk and positive thinking. This young woman first told me how fortunate I was that I grew up in a home where my parents always talked positive to and about me and raised me to do the same. I fully agreed with her. This young lady then went on to tell me she had never been a positive thinker and also never spoke positively. She told me that many people in her life tell her that she is always very negative. Although this young girl was living with spina bifida and facing many challenges around that issue, she also was a bright, articulate young woman who had much potential. It broke my heart that she was limiting her true potential and quality of life in such a substantial way because of her life of negativity.

She told me that after hearing me talk about the impact of positive self-talk, she wanted to change and she wanted to start becoming more positive in her words and thoughts. But she told me, "Shauna, after years of being so negative, I don't know how or where to begin to be more positive."

I told her the best wisdom I could give her in just the few minutes I had was that it starts with one thought and one word at a time. I suggested that the next time she hears herself saying something negative or thinking negatively, to just stop right there and change those words or that thought into something that is true and positive and believe it. If she would do this first step, she would be on her way to changing the quality of her life.

The truth is that getting our words and thoughts lined up for success does take discipline until it becomes natural and normal. It is a matter of creating habitual ways of speaking and thinking. If negative self-talk has been normal for you for a long time, you won't be totally transformed by tomorrow. Consistent discipline and effort will lead to a lifetime of change; that change is something worth the effort and discipline.

And the best advice I can give you about changing your self-talk is simply to never say something to yourself that you would not say to anyone else. If you would not tell your mother, child, or best friend what you are saying to yourself, *you should not be saying it!* Becoming your own best friend rather than your own worst critic will go a long way in helping you change your self-talk!

It is my hope that from this chapter, you have truly come to realize the impact your words and thoughts have on the quality of your life. I hope you have found that even though you may be going through some challenging circumstances in your life, there are solutions that will help you lead a more successful and fulfilled life. One of those solutions is by simply changing your words.

CHAPTER 4

New Beginnings!

"Should you shield the canyons from the windstorms, you would never see the beauty of their carvings"—Elisabeth Kübler-Ross, MD.

"Disappointment to a noble soul is what cold water means to burning metal; it strengthens, tempers, intensifies, but never destroys it"—Eliza Tabor.

"When one door closes another door opens; but we so often look so long and so regretfully upon the closed door, that we do not see the ones which open for us"—Alexander Graham Bell.

We all have faced pain, disappointment, loss, hardship, and obstacles that can seem impossible to overcome. These things are an inevitable part of our journey through life. We all face challenges we did not create and things happen in life that are beyond our control. However, the key that will take us from merely surviving or just existing in the midst of adversity and pain lies in our choosing. Choice, I believe is what determines if we will let our pain destroy our dreams and our future or if we will learn and grow and only become better despite our challenges and pain. God has given all of us the amazing ability to choose in our life; it is called free will. We all have pain, but we also have the awesome ability to choose every day what we will do with that pain. The difference between those who are able to soar above their adversities compared to those who become stuck in their obstacles, lies in their choosing and in their attitude.

In his book, *LIFE: Living in Freedom Every Day,* Kenneth Brown says, "It's been said that a setback is nothing more than a set-up for a comeback. With the right attitude, the setbacks you face teach you new things and make you stronger. You come back bigger and better than you were."

I know for certain that my family and I would not be who we are spiritually, emotionally, or mentally had I not been born with spina bifida. Spina bifida only made all of us stronger and better. Struggle and pain has a way of either making you dig deeper and become more than you were before the struggle or, if you choose to let it, your struggles can dominate you and make you become less than you were before the struggle.

When I was born with spina bifida and the doctors told my parents they did not know if I would ever walk or if I would even live, that unknown and uncertain future led my family and me (as I got older) into finding God and His Truth, as well as a deeper meaning in life. The circumstances of spina bifida led us down our wonderful spiritual journeys. We may have never embarked upon those journeys had we not had to face the many uncertain circumstances of my condition.

Many times, adversity forces us to find and use resources we have never used before. Through adversity in life, I found my strongest resources in God, spiritual truth, my mind, the depth of my spirit and inner resilience, as well as the amazing wisdom of my parents. However, it is my spiritual foundation in God that has been the driving force for everything in my life. I always knew that no matter what my physical circumstances were, God was always greater than those circumstances; His plan for my life was much bigger than my physical circumstances. Had I not had those challenges, I don't know how long it would have taken for me to find and know the spiritual truths that I now base my entire life upon.

I was once asked at a seminar an interesting question: If I could choose to not have been born with spina bifida, would I choose to not have it? My answer was absolutely not! I know it is the life of living with spina bifida that made me the compassionate, strong, kind, joyful, positive, spiritual person that I am. Had I not had this struggle to shape me and form me into the person I am today, I have no idea what type of person I would have turned out to be. I am thankful for my journey and life just as it is—even with all of its tremendous difficulties. I am proud of who I am today and what I have accomplished in my life. I view spina bifida as a catalyst that moved me into a deeper and more meaningful life. Living with spina bifida made me learn at a very early age what really mattered in life. I had to learn to embrace life for what it was so that I could fulfill my purpose on this Earth.

I absolutely love what Napoleon Hill says in his book, *A Year of Growing Rich,* "Struggle . . . toughens the human spirit. Most people try to go through life following the path of least resistance. They fail to recognize that this philosophy is what make's rivers crooked—and sometimes does the same things for human beings. Without the strength of character that grows out of struggle, we would be mightily tempted to flow through life with little purpose or plan. "

He goes on to say, "Every adversity, every failure, and every unpleasant experience carries with it the seed of an equivalent benefit, which may prove a blessing in disguise."

I truly believe that every adverse circumstance is a catalyst for change. We can let our adverse circumstances lead us into a deeper understanding of how our life should be and use it as a teacher and motivator, or we can stay lost in our struggle and pain. But in order for us to move into the new things in our life that our challenging circumstances can lead us into, we have to be willing to let go of our old struggles and be willing to embrace what the circumstance is trying to shape us into. By using every event as a catalyst to bring us into greater understanding, we then can turn the negative things in our lives into something positive, transform our pain into peace, our turmoil into triumph, and our emotional wounds into wisdom.

43

My late brother, Shad, was such an example of honor and integrity to me in my life. In 2007, my family and I had to watch him go through extreme adversity. Watching him taught me so very much about living. In the summer of 2007, only six months after my brother's life-threatening and life-altering motorcycle accident, his wife of nine years told him she wanted a divorce. Shad's world came crashing down. He had thought his wife was his best friend and the love of his life.

After the divorce, Shad had to endure much loneliness, depression, and heartache. However, being the amazing person he was, he began to pull himself out of his despair and began to look for the lessons in this extremely painful experience.

At the end of 2007, a friend of his, asked him, "When was the best year of your life?"

"This year!" Shad answered.

My brother's friend thought he had lost his mind. "Dude, you were in a horrible motorcycle accident this year, which was not your fault. You almost died and your wife of nine years left you!"

In his amazing wisdom Shad said, "Yeah, but I also learned so much about myself this year. I grew so much and I learned to forgive and forgive myself, so it was the best year of my life."

Shad gained so very much from his experiences of 2007 because he chose too. He could have held on to the pain and heartache and become bitter and angry and imprisoned in his circumstances, but he didn't. He chose the high road, not only for himself, but also for his ex-wife and all of those around him. He therefore came out of those horrible situations better than he was before.

What is so truly beautiful about this story is at the end of that horrible year of 2007, Shad also met the real love of his life—Autumn. The kind of love my brother and Autumn had was like nothing either of them had ever known before. My brother found something so much greater than he had ever expected after all of that loss and heartache, and I truly believe that is because my brother kept moving forward; he did not give up. He did not surrender to the anger or pain or become a victim of unfair events. He chose to grow and learn, and on the other side of all that pain he found something so much more beautiful than he had ever known before. Autumn was the most beautiful gift Shad could ever have been given. Their love was something many spend a lifetime looking for. But had my brother chosen the lower road of victimhood, anger, and unforgiveness, he probably would never have found Autumn and never would have known the amazing love they shared.

My brother's story is why I want to tell you how vital it is that we keep learning and growing and become better in the midst of our adversity. I truly believe that if we will do so, we have no idea what amazing things could be waiting for us on the other side of our adversity and pain.

In Debbie Ford's book, *The Right Questions,* she wisely instructs us to "See your triumphs and tragedies as invitations to evolve and grow." She also says "It is precisely at the moments of greatest challenge that we need to look beyond what we can see and find a deeper meaning in them." I think that statement is so true because when we can find the deeper true meaning of our circumstances, that is when we will find freedom, hope, empowerment, and forgiveness. When we get to the point where we can "use everything to our advantage," as spiritual teacher Muktananda says, that is when we truly become empowered and are no longer ruled by our circumstances.

Failure, defeat, and pain very often can open doors to new and greater opportunities, and really can become blessings in disguise! I think it is safe to say that most of the greatest transformations, achievements, and growth in our personal lives come from life's disappointments and adversities. If we are open to growth and new beginnings, pain and adversity can force us to change our course in life so that we can arrive at greater joy, wisdom, fulfillment, and opportunities. It has been said that "God never shuts a door without opening a window." We must look for the windows in our lives because right outside that window could be something so much more wonderful than anything we have ever seen!

I have a very dear friend who, when her son was a teenager, he became part of a suicide pact in his high school. Unfortunately, he did take his life right in front of his family's home. As horrific and hard as this situation was for my dear friend and her family, whenever we spoke about the situation, she always told me that although she did lose her precious son that day, it was her son's suicide that caused every other teenager involved in that suicide pact to make the decision to live and not take their own lives. So, the suicide of my dear friend's son saved many other teenagers' lives that year. The lessons and wisdom learned in this horrible situation brought about life-changing events for many other families.

I think it is safe to say that some of the most profound changes that have come about in our history, culture, society, communities, and personal lives have come as a result of adversities that required us to learn, grow, and change. Many of the regulations, laws, and organizations in place today are in place because of adversities or losses occurring in which people saw the need to change things for the better and did so.

Many of today's changes would never have occurred had something or someone not been lost to begin with.

An example is Oprah's current huge movement to get pledges signed to stop text messaging while driving. Hearing about the preventable deaths that have occurred while people were driving and texting started her movement. Those losses are also the cause of the many laws and bans we now have in place regarding texting and driving.

There are many organizations in our culture that have been formed because of adversity such as MADD. I love hearing stories of people who have lost something or someone, yet saw the opportunity to give something back to society because of their circumstances. That kind of love and giving in the midst of pain and challenges only makes life better for all of us. When we can take our circumstances and make them into something that adds value to our own or others' lives, then we have mastered our circumstances rather than allowing them to master us.

That level of transformation in the midst of suffering also holds the possibility of creating a whole new purpose for living in the lives of those touched by adversity. It is possible to find renewed purpose from the things that are our greatest challenges—if we allow ourselves to be open to that level of transformation.

Crime crusader John Walsh is a great example of this. John and his wife, Reve, founded the National Center for Missing and Exploited Children as well as their popular television show *America's Most Wanted*. The organization and television show were founded after losing their six-year-old son to a horrible murder by a pedophile in 1981.

Although I don't know either of them personally, I do know that had John Walsh and his wife chosen the route of bitterness, anger, and victimhood in this situation, they probably would never have been able to see how they could turn their horrible pain and loss into something that has now brought justice and freedom to the lives of many. Many children have been saved from suffering at the hands of sexual predators because of John and Reve Walsh's work. And we are all better and safer because the Walsh's choice to allow their suffering and loss lead them into an entirely new purpose that has affected the lives of many!

Victor Frankl's story of how he survived and overcame time spent in a Nazi concentration camp, as well as the loss of his entire family, has always greatly inspired me. I love this quote of his: "Man's main concern is not to gain pleasure or to avoid pain but rather to see a meaning in his life. That is why man is even ready to suffer, on a condition, to be sure that his suffering has a meaning." Suffering truly can bring about greater meaning in our lives, but we have to be willing to embrace the new meaning and purpose in order to find our freedom.

I observed such a powerful witness today to the message I want to express in this chapter about the importance of discovering the opportunities in the midst of our pain and challenges. My husband is easily touched and moved by positive people. This is one reason why we love each other so much. My husband and I had just seen a clip from YouTube of the amazing man Nick Vujicic who was born without arms and legs and is also a very powerful motivational-inspirational speaker.

My husband showed this clip to an old friend of his who had stopped by our house. His friend struggles with many health problems, yet he also contributes a lot to those problems by way of his behavior.

My husband and his friend listened to Nick speak. Nick shared his belief in the amazing truth that he didn't need arms and legs to love or raise a child, if that is ever part of his future, because he had a heart to love a child, which is all that is really needed.

After hearing Nick share that, my husband's friend started proclaiming all of the negative things he could see in raising a child without arms or legs and how very hard it would be to do. My husband's friend could not see what Nick sees in his own life. Nick sees the opportunities in his life in the midst of extreme challenges. Can a person raise wonderful children, even without arms and legs? Of course! Nick believes he can and he understands that it is not just physical abilities that can impact a life. What makes the greatest difference in the lives around us is what comes from our hearts! Nick has chosen a way of life of focusing on what he does have and that attitude is what has taken him to where he is today.

After my husband's friend left I told my husband that I would not be where I am today and probably wouldn't even be alive if I had only focused on what I couldn't do in life and what was wrong with me or my situations. I told him I felt it was the same for Nick. Had he spent his life focusing on his limitations and how horrible his life was without arms and legs, who knows where he would have ended up? Yet, Nick has already gone so very far in his young life, all because of what he has chosen to believe, see, and focus on.

I truly believe that if my husband's friend would choose to be more positive and see the possibilities in his trying circumstances, he would be a much healthier man and probably have a much better quality of life.

What we choose to focus on determines so much in our lives. Because Nick Vujicic has chosen to focus on all of the positive things he can see, he is motivating, inspiring, and changing the world, one speech at a time. Nick is undoubtedly making the world a brighter place because of embracing the opportunities in front of him, even in the midst of extreme adversity.

Adversity has the ability to make us stop, look, and listen to that still small voice as well as read the signs that could be leading us down a new path in our lives. Adversity is usually a signal that some part of our lives has come to an end or needs to come to an end. Adversity gives us the opportunity to evaluate life patterns that are no longer working, as well as develop new attitudes about our relationships, ourselves, money, our health, our vocation or career, as well as our ambitions, values, and passions. Adversity causes us to literally take inventory. Taking inventory and listening and looking for the greater opportunity are what hold the power to move us out of our place of suffering into a place of freedom. We must be willing to look beyond where we are right now to see new possibilities, be open to new ideas, and expect great things in our future. We must be open to what we cannot see and don't understand in order to make room for what is in our future.

I believe God always wants us to rise higher. He wants us to let go of anything that would hold us captive. Trying to hold on to what we had with clenched fists only robs us of the freedom that is waiting ahead for us. When we are willing to let go of our old struggles, we

49

will find our greatest inner strength as well as the person we were really meant to be. I believe there is always another chapter of our lives waiting for us, but we have to be willing to walk into it.

Part of moving beyond adversity into finding true freedom also often involves forgiving others and/or forgiving yourself. Adversity's ultimate purpose is to cause us to learn and grow, and sometimes that learning and growing is from past mistakes and learning to move on with dignity, hope, confidence, integrity, and faith. However, if forgiveness or self-forgiveness is necessary for you to move forward and you aren't able to do so, you will be carrying those circumstances and lack of forgiveness into every future situation, relationship, action, and decision. To forgive yourself and others and really let go of whatever past mistakes or pain is keeping you stuck is truly one of the greatest gifts you can give yourself and anyone who may have hurt you. It is impossible to truly move forward in life unless we are able to bring closure to the events of the past that may be holding us back. Forgiveness of others or self-forgiveness is not condoning past mistakes, it is simply allowing you or the other person(s) to be free from the pain and prison of the past. We all have had people hurt us in life and we have all made mistakes, but if we refuse to let go of those things and refuse to offer forgiveness, we will only suffer more. Lack of forgiveness for yourself or others is like feeding a monster in your life. As one of my great friends used to say, "Don't feed the monster!"

My parents always said it is one thing to make a mistake, because we all make them, yet it is another to keep making the same mistakes over and over. We are only headed down a dead end road because we haven't learned from them. Alexander Pope said "To err is human, to forgive divine." If you really want to be free in your life, you have to get rid of any old junk that would hold you back. Holding on to past resentments, anger, or unforgiveness for others or yourself will only poison your life and keep you from where you want to go.

So, how can we truly begin to tap into new opportunities in the midst of adverse circumstances? The key is to look for the potential that exists within the obstacle. One of the greatest tools to help transform you from a place of despair and hopelessness into freedom is to ask yourself, "What could be right about the obstacle in my life?" Discovering what could be right about what seems so wrong in your life will take you into a place of being proactive in your life rather than reactive, which will then allow you to discover how you need to move forward out of your adversity. When all we do is react to the negative situations in our lives rather than look for the opportunities and possibilities, then we simply become defeated and a victim of our circumstances. In the Chinese language, two brush strokes are used to write the word "crisis." One stroke represents danger, the opportunity. To me, it is all about what we choose to see when we are faced with trying circumstances.

Some other pivotal questions to ask yourself when in the midst of adverse circumstances are:

"What can I learn from this encounter?"

"What opportunities do I see in this challenge?"

"How can I use this situation to transform my life?"

"Do I have a problem with the possibility of meeting a great need for humanity if the problem is solved?"

Asking these questions when you feel lost and imprisoned in your circumstances will begin to help you change your perspective and help you move from a place of focusing on what is wrong and how bad your situation is to the new possibilities you may have been searching for all along.

J. Sidlo Baxter has said, "What is the difference between an obstacle and an opportunity? Our attitude toward it. Every opportunity has a difficulty, and every difficulty has an opportunity." Lou Holtz has said "Show me someone who has done something worthwhile and I will show you someone who has overcome adversity."

I think a wonderful promise you could make to yourself in the midst of adversity would be: "I will not live in defeat and disappointment because of setbacks and/or struggles. I am not going to dwell on yesterday's disappointments and I refuse to be trapped in the past. A dream or plan may have died, but today I promise myself to dream a new dream."

I want to end with the final part of a poem in Tim Connors book, *The Basics of Success*. The poem is called "Know How to Overcome Failure." The last part of that poem says:

"Failure [or adversity] is not negative. It is a teacher. It molds, refines, and polishes you so that one day your light will shine for all to see. It isn't the failure [or adversity] you experience that will determine your destiny, but your next step and then the next that will tell the story of your life."

My greatest hope for you is that you will take the next step in the story of your life out of adversity and into your genuine freedom.

CHAPTER 5

DISCOVERING PEACE, FINDING HOPE, AND CREATING JOY!

"How you see things on the outside of you depends on how things are on the inside of you"—John L. Mason from *Let Go of Whatever Makes You Stop.*

"What oxygen is to the lungs, such is hope to the meaning of life"—Emil Brunner.

Peace, hope, and joy are truly vital components to our quality of life and well-being. They are what enable us to cope with whatever situations we are facing. Peace, hope, and joy lift us to new places mentally, emotionally, and spiritually and take us out of our anger, disappointment, and heartache. Peace, hope, and joy can be found in many different places for all of us, yet because they are vital to our well-being, I want to explore with you in this chapter how to go about discovering true peace in the midst of tragedy, hope in the midst of loss, and joy even in the midst of pain.

Discovering Peace

Someone once said: "Serenity is not freedom from the storm, but peace amid the storm." But how do we go about finding peace in the midst of the storms of life? Our outward perspective or attitude in life has a direct affect on our level of inner peace. However, our inner attitudes also have a lot to do with our outer perspective. It has been said that: "peace is a state of mind, as is suffering, so if our mind is peaceful, we will be happy." I personally believe that true peace comes from within us and not from outside us.

But what is peace, exactly? One of Webster's definitions of peace is, "inner contentment, serenity." Another is, "a state of calm and quiet." My favorite definition is, "freedom from disturbing thoughts or emotions." So, really, peace is the opposite of inner conflict, stress, or feeling anxious. Peace also is: "without war or fighting." You can apply this definition to your mental state and/or emotions because when you are fighting against anything in life, whether it is yourself, circumstances, God, or others, you are not at peace.

Even though it can seem impossible to find genuine peace in the midst of the trials and storms of life, I know it is possible. I have found true inner peace despite living with daily physical struggles from spina bifida and experiencing pain and loss in my life. My personal inner peace has come primarily from God, who is the "Prince of Peace" (Isaiah 9:6) and who promises us the "Peace of God, which surpasses all understanding" (Philippians 4:7).

That last scripture is meaningful to me because from our human perspective, when we see someone who struggles daily with health and physical issues, it is easy to think, how can that person truly have peace? I can honestly tell you that the peace I live with is beyond understanding because it comes from God whose peace resides within me!

I dearly love the words of "The Serenity Prayer" by Reinhold Niebuhr: "God grant me the serenity to accept the things I cannot change, the courage to change the things I can; and the wisdom to know the difference." I have prayed this prayer many times when I have felt stuck in circumstances in my life.

It takes acknowledgement, courage, and perseverance to actually change the things we know we can change in life. It also takes faith, strength, and patience to genuinely accept the things we cannot change. It takes emotional maturity to stop resisting those things we don't want in life, but can't change. To stop wanting to change the things we cannot change is not giving up, it is simply seeing your life and circumstances more clearly.

One of the prime causes of suffering is from wanting things to be different than they are, so it is vital in discovering peace of mind that we learn to accept the things we cannot change in life.

It also takes wisdom to know the difference between what we can and cannot change. Many times we so desperately want circumstances in our lives to be different that we spend all of our time regretting, being angry, and trying to change things of which we have no control, that we actually become more stuck in our pain rather than finding peace. Then we never find the momentum to actually change what we can change in our lives because we are wasting so much energy and giving all of our power away to things we cannot change, rather than allowing ourselves to heal and just accept them.

When we come to a place of truly accepting what we cannot change in life, yet find the courage to change the things we can, this is truly when we find real inner peace. I really try to remember "The Serenity Prayer" when I find myself losing peace over a circumstance. If I find myself upset over something, I try to ask myself, "Can I change this?" If I can't change it, I have to learn to accept it as it is and go on. However, if I can change it, I look for the solution to the problem and start working on that rather than allowing the circumstance to control me or steal my peace or joy.

Being born with spina bifida and my brother's death are both things that no matter how much I wanted to, I could never change. Being able to accept these things and yet find the courage to change the things I can were critical components for me in discovering true inner peace. Even though I have many physical issues from spina bifida, to live with true inner peace, I have had to accept myself and my body as it is and realize that although my body is not what anyone would consider "perfect," I am an amazing creation of God and I have a purpose for my life, despite my physical difficulties.

These realizations were the first step in my finding deep, abiding inner peace. Our own self-esteem and level of respect for ourselves as amazing creations of God, full of unlimited potential has a tremendous affect on our level of true inner peace. When we can come to a place of fully understanding "The Serenity Prayer," it provides us the ability to actually let go of the regret, anger, disappointment, and pain that can keep us stuck in our circumstances. We can then move on to new things in life and be able to live in our true and most fulfilling purpose.

I love what Naomi Judd says in her book *Naomi's Breakthrough Guide:* "It's actually the significance that you and I attach to our experiences, and then the way we choose to incorporate the lessons into our future, that make us either more fulfilled or worse off than before." There always is another way of looking at things; changing your perspective can do wonders for bringing you peace of mind.

One of my dear friends recently displayed such an example of true inner peace to me. She was recently in a serious accident with her horse. Her horses and roping have been her life, throughout her life. She had even expressed to me that she "is nothing without her horses." However, after her accident she expressed to me that she does not know if she will ever ride again because her injuries were quite extensive. When I asked her how she was dealing with that fact, since her true love in life is her horses, she explained to me that she is planning on taking up another hobby and that she sees this experience as maybe something that is taking her in a new direction in her life.

I was truly amazed at my friend's peace of mind at possibly having to give up the thing she has loved the most in life. In the midst of that loss, she is seeing the new opportunities and embracing them; in the midst of that, she has found true inner peace.

Other things we can do to discover and foster peace in our lives are actually quite simple; however, when we are looking at our lives through the lens of pain, anger, or heartache, it can be very difficult to see the solutions to our turmoil.

One of the first things you can do to begin to experience peace is to find or create a solution(s) to the circumstances that are causing you pain, anger, or anxiety. When you believe a solution has been discovered and is possible, the problem is not nearly as big as it seemed without a solution.

Letting go of any negative thoughts and/or emotions such as anger and guilt that you may be harboring in relation to your painful or challenging circumstances is critical, especially in circumstances over which you have no control. You may not even be aware of negative thoughts or feelings that you may be harboring, so you may need to take inventory of your thought life to determine if you are thinking too many negative thoughts that are keeping you stuck or holding you back from where you really want to be. If true peace of mind is where you want to be, holding on to anger, regret, or guilt will never take you there!

Another solution is simply doing what you enjoy doing. Doing what you love truly does lead to peace within. I absolutely believe we were all created for a unique purpose that only we can fulfill. When we get lost in our circumstances and get off track with our purpose, it can cause us to lose so much peace. Reconnecting with your purpose and doing what makes you happiest can do wonders for restoring peace in your life. If your adversity has taken you so far off the path that you don't even know what your purpose is anymore, some questions you can ask yourself to help you discover what you were made for are:

- What are your greatest strengths right now?

- What absolutely makes your heart sing?

- What are you drawn to?

- What comes easily to you?

- What do people in your life praise you for?

Considering the answers to your questions can help you find what you enjoy most and help get you back on the path of your most fulfilling purpose.

It is also essential that we learn to build healthy relationships based on respect, confidence, and purpose. This includes healthy relationships with yourself, God, and others. When we are at odds with anyone, including ourselves, we will not experience true peace, no matter how hard we try to. It is essential that you arrive at a place of peace and respect for yourself and others, regardless of your past circumstances.

It is also important, especially in the case of loss and grief, that you celebrate good memories. Remembering those you love and may have lost will keep their memory alive in your hearts, which can bring you more peace. I don't know that we ever stop missing the loved ones we have lost, bur remembering how much they added to our life and the life of others while they were here on this Earth can go a long way in restoring peace in our lives.

Learning to truly live in the moment, also known as mindfulness, is a vital solution to creating more peace. The reason mindfulness is essential to discovering true, abiding peace is that when we place so much emphasis on what has happened (the past) in our lives, or are constantly worried about the future, it becomes impossible to experience the peace of right now. We spend so much of our lives living either in the past or the future that we lose what we have right now. To discover peace, it is vital that we learn how to live for the moment of right now and embrace where we are today.

Stephen R. Covey, in his book, *Daily Reflections for Highly Effective People,* wrote: "Whatever is at the center of our life will be our source of security, guidance, wisdom, and power." So, it is vital in discovering peace that you determine what is most essential to you in your life and what the center of your life is, because what is central to you determines where you will go in your life and how much peace you will have.

In discovering peace, it is of utmost importance that we trust that we will have the inner strength to create something good from our circumstances and that we know we can live a fulfilling life-even in the midst of hardship. We must know and truly believe that we can rise above our circumstances and that we can find true inner peace and purpose.

Finding hope

Zig Ziglar has said, "There are seldom, if ever, any hopeless situations, but there are many people who lose hope in the face of some situations." It can be very easy for us to lose hope in the midst of our challenging situations. However, when we can see our situations clearly, we discover that there really are no circumstances in life that are actually hopeless. This can take time, some introspection, and a change in perspective to begin to see your challenging situations from a clearer vantage point that can be full of hope. This is why I think it is so important to discuss this topic in this book.

But what is hope exactly? Webster's Dictionary defines it several ways. My two favorite definitions are: "To desire with expectation of fulfillment," and "One that gives promise for the future."

Our expectations for the future are in direct correlation to the level of hope we have. When we expect good things to happen, it does give us hope for living, regardless of the circumstances we are facing. Hope is the belief that a positive outcome lies ahead and that we will arrive at something new in our lives.

In his book, *20/20 Vision*, Bishop Jim Earl Swilley wrote, "Hope is the effectual combination of expectation and desire...on some level you only get what you expect to get out of your circumstances... Expecting good things to happen is a healthy habit that can easily be developed and can elevate the quality of your life."

You may have just been through or are experiencing a very tough situation, but what are you expecting for your future in the midst of your challenges? Take some time and do some inventory of your thoughts and expectations for your future. What could be lying ahead for you in the midst of your struggle that may take you to a brand new place in your life?

Hope is a way of thinking, feeling, and living that may help us to discover new ways to live with our difficult situations. Believing in yourself, your abilities, the unique purpose you were created for, and getting rid of self-doubt are also vital in finding hope.

Through all of my daily struggles of living with a permanent disability, I don't even see or "live in" those struggles. I have always believed God is forever with me. I believe His favor is upon my life and He gives me the strength I need to deal with my circumstances. My hope has always come from my faith in God and His plan for my life, which I always knew was much bigger than my circumstances. I have always believed that because of God's presence and power in my life, I would live a blessed and fulfilling life, regardless of my physical challenges.

In his book, *A Year of Growing Rich,* Napoleon Hill wrote, "Hope is the raw material with which you build success. It crystallizes into faith, faith into determination, and determination into action." Having just one ounce of hope can literally transform a person's life from being lost in hurt, anger, or grief. One ounce of hope can catapult a person's life into an entirely new direction—that is how powerful hope is!

Hope is a very important coping mechanism, and causes us to keep moving forward in life. Hope is being honest with ourselves about our situations, yet still looking forward to positive possible outcomes in our future.

I love what Naomi Judd says in her book, *Naomi's Breakthrough Guide, "HOPE [acronym] is the Healing Of Painful Experiences."*

When you have found hope, you have found healing! When we can find the good in every situation, regardless of how hard the circumstances are, we also find hope.

How do we learn to foster hope in our live, when the world looks the darkest and we are faced with hardship or tragedy? Hope is something we can build in each other through the attentiveness we show to each other. Hope is a benefit of our attentiveness because when we know that our existence is enhancing the life of others, it creates hope within us.

It is also important that you remember and reconnect with what has brought you hope in the past. This can be something that brought you hope many years ago in childhood, or something that brought you hope in a more recent past—last year or last month.

You must also talk about and verbalize the things you expect in your life and the happy endings you see in your life. I mentioned the importance of self-talk earlier. Talking about what you expect and want in your life keeps hope alive in you. Remember, whatever you talk about gets stronger and the messages you tell yourself when you are at your lowest are a big part of what determines how fast you will get back up again. So, when you talk about your hope and faith and verbalize your expectations and optimism, the more real the things you are talking about become.

Talk about your dreams. To keep moving forward, as a result of your hope and faith, decide on a definite goal you would love to accomplish; then write it down, commit it to memory, and make it the guiding light to direct you into your new future!

Thomas J. Peters says: "You must celebrate what you want to see more of!" You must dare to dream big dreams and don't accept any limitations! I didn't accept limitations in my life and that is a big part of what kept hope alive in me! Believe that truly nothing is impossible for you, because you were destined for greatness and you do have the power to succeed! In doing these things, it is my desire and prayer you will find the hope you may have been longing for!

Discovering Joy

I love this quote by John MacArthur: "God made you. He knows how you operate best. And He knows what makes you happy. The happiness He gives doesn't stop when the party's over. It lasts because it comes from deep within." We are learning from the wisdom of this chapter, that peace, hope and joy do not come from external factors, they come from within. So no matter what you are going through, you can live a life of peace, hope, and joy!

Monique Nicole Nance said, "I believe God, through His Spirit, grants us love, joy and peace no matter what is happening in our lives. . . . we shouldn't expect our joy to always feel like happiness, but instead recognize joy as inner security."

I have always loved the scripture, Nehemiah 8:10, "The Joy of the Lord is your strength." I have been told all my life that I am full of joy and am always so happy, positive, and bubbly. I do believe I was given the gift of joy and it truly is my strength in life. I have met people, though, who do not understand my deep level of joy. In one of my seminars, as someone saw me walk and observed what I have to deal with physically, and yet saw my joy, he referred to me as a "Pollyanna." However, I know where my joy comes from, and it absolutely is genuine joy.

My joy truly comes from within, from what the Lord has put inside of me. My parents even joke that, "I came out telling the doctor a joke." But my deep, abiding joy is also a daily choice. I know I could choose to live my life depressed, angry, or as a victim of my circumstances, however, that is not the life I want to live. I chose many years ago to live my life to the fullest and I want to live my life as joyful as possible.

In his book, *30 Thoughts for Victorious Living*, Joel Osteen wrote: "When you are full of joy and have a good attitude, you keep yourself strong." I absolutely agree with that statement. I know my deep, abiding joy has taken me much further in life than self-pity, anger, or depression ever would have.

Let me ask you, are you happy, are you a joyful person? If you aren't, what would it take for you to become joyful and happy? What would it take for joy and happiness to become your lifestyle? The good news is, because we have more control of our lives than we even think, we can choose a life of joy and happiness regardless of what is going on around us. How is this possible? It's because we can choose and control our words, social situations, responses, attitudes, and physical environment.

But what is joy? While happiness is a state of being, joy is the emotional response we display to the state of being happy. Our joy is expressed through our joyous speech, laughter, our smiles, and other joy-filled responses.

In his book, *Deadly Emotions,* Dr. Don Colbert wrote, "Joy . . . is abiding and enduring. It comes from a feeling of contentment deep inside a person. It is not dependent on external factors, but on an inner sense of value, purpose, fulfillment, or satisfaction." This is my favorite description of joy. This description clearly makes the point that joy is not a result of external circumstances but rather it comes from within. Dr. Colbert also wrote, "Joy does not flow from situations. It flows from your will and your emotions deep within. You can choose to be joyful, or you can choose to be miserable. Nobody can make these inner choices for you."

So how can we begin to create more joy in our lives? One of the greatest ways to create joy in our life is through laughter. In high school I competed in the speech team. During my junior year, I wrote and competed using a ten-minute oratory speech on the "Healing Power of Laughter." I *loved* giving that speech because it was something I believed to my core. I did so well with it that I qualified for Nationals and had the opportunity to compete with other orators from across the nation. In doing all of my research for that speech, I learned much about laughter and its healing benefits.

In Proverbs 17:22 it is written, "A merry heart does good like medicine." Laughter can go a long way in creating more joy in our lives and to improving our physical health. Loma Linda University Medical Center's Dr. Lee Berk has written about the health and healing benefits of laughter. Through his studies, he came to the conclusion that laughter boosts the immune system and reduces dangerous stress hormones in the body. Cortisol (the primary stress hormone) has a very serious affect on our bodies.

In his book, *Deadly Emotions,* Dr Don Colbert wrote: "Berk's findings about cortisol are especially important. Cortisol is the dangerous stress hormone that, once elevated for extended periods of time, can act like acid in the body. It especially affects the brain, eventually causing memory loss." Cortisol also affects our immune system, inflammation levels, and it can also lead to many health issues such as heart attacks, arthritis, infections, bone loss, back aches, cancer, headaches, and many other illnesses.

When we are constantly angered, stressed, or upset, it seriously affects our body and physical health. Laughter is an excellent prescription for greater health and increased joy.

In his book, *Your Best Life Now,* Joel Osteen wrote, ". . . people who are happy and have a positive outlook, people who laugh on a regular basis, develop more of these natural killer cells than the average person." (Natural killer cells are the cells that attack and destroy abnormal cells.) So, when we live a life of joy, our immune system can function at its optimum level.

Laughter has even been described by Dr. William Fry Jr. as being as good as exercise. Laughing one hundred to two hundred times a day is equal to ten minutes of rowing or jogging. Other researchers say that twenty seconds of belly laughter is equal to three minutes of working out on a rowing machine (from W. F. Fry, *Make 'Em Laugh*). Humor expert Patty Wooten has said that: "The average adult laughs twenty-five times a day and the average child four hundred times a day"! Isn't that shocking!

I love the story of Victor Frankl and I have mentioned him earlier. Victor Frankl was a psychiatrist and survivor of the Auschwitz concentration camp. He has written that humor was a critical component to his survival in there. As a prisoner, Frankl encouraged his fellow prisoners to tell funny stories about the things they intended to do when they were released. In his writings, Frankl wrote, "I never would have made it if I could not have laughed. It lifted me momentarily out of this horrible situation, just enough to make it livable."

So how can we begin to laugh more? It begins with smiling more. Dr. Don Colbert wrote, "Laughter starts on the heels of smiling" *(Deadly Emotions)*. Laughter and smiling are results of an emotional state, but they can also create an emotional state—that of joy! Joel Osteen also wrote, "One of the healthiest things you can do is learn to smile more often. When we smile, it sends a message to our whole body . . . Studies tell us when we smile, certain chemicals are released that travel throughout our system, relaxing us and helping us stay healthy" *(Your Best Life Now)*.

If you are having a hard time finding a reason to smile, here are some tips:

- Hug a child or someone else you love.

- Find your baby pictures.

- Watch some of your favorite cartoons or comedians.

- Visit a pet store or a humane society.

I think a great life-long prescription for joy would be to practice smiling and laughing every day.

Doing things to put a smile on another person's face can also do wonders for bringing greater joy to you and the other person as well. It creates a ripple effect of happiness in the world. Joy is contagious, so when you share it with others, it spreads like wildfire. I truly believe that the more joy you give away, whether it be in smiles or laughter, you will experience and receive more joy.

Another way to create more joy in our lives is to just learn to have more fun—to lighten up! Life can be very short. I had to learn this hard lesson when my brother passed away when he was only thirty-two and when I lost a nephew who was only nine months old. When our time is up on this Earth, I don't think any of us will ever say, "I wish I had worked more, been angrier or more sad, seen fewer places, learned less or loved less." No, we will say, "I wish I had enjoyed life more, worked less, seen more, learned more, and loved more." When you have fun in life, you are better able to face the struggles, challenges, and trials that life can throw you.

Many of us as adults are afraid to lighten up or act "silly." But I absolutely love what Dr. Colbert wrote: "Are you aware that the word 'silly' comes from the Greek word 'selig,' which means 'blessed'?" (*Deadly Emotions*). That is beautiful! To act lighthearted and joyous is to actually be blessed! How many of us could use more blessings in our lives?

It is vital to your health and well-being that you do things you enjoy doing and do them often. If you are at a place where you don't even know what you enjoy anymore, remind yourself of what you used to enjoy. What did you enjoy doing during happier times or when you were a child? It is important that you reconnect with those things that have brought you joy in the past. If you can no longer do what used to bring you joy, maybe it is time to take up a new hobby or find something new that can bring you joy. Pursue what you enjoy with passion. Having a purpose and passion for something that has meaning and value are what get you up in the morning and keep you moving forward in life.

The last and probably most important nugget of wisdom I want to share with you is to not allow circumstances to steal your joy. So often we don't lose our joy, we simply give it away. We give our joy to our circumstances and other people, which is essentially giving our power away; this only causes us to lose out. When we let our circumstances control or dictate our emotions, that circumstance becomes the driver of our lives. The circumstance or person we gave our power away to take charge of our lives rather than our being in charge of our lives. Then we are just basically people being tossed around by life rather than being in control of our lives! I will never let spina bifida or any other circumstance tell me who I am or dictate my life by any means.

I do live a life of true freedom even in the midst of many physical challenges, and it is my hope that this book has helped you learn how you could live a life of that genuine freedom too, despite any circumstance you have faced in the past, are facing, or have to face in the future! God bless you and thank you for joining me on this journey of sharing with you my life's story!

CHAPTER 6

CLOSING THOUGHTS

"What the caterpillar calls the end of the world, the master calls a butterfly"—Richard Bach.

The primary intent of this book was about helping you as the reader transform your life from one of struggle, hardship, and pain into true freedom—even in the midst of painful or challenging circumstances.

Life can be extremely challenging at times and we all do go through difficult situations in life, but we don't have to let those situations break us or hold us back from living the life we were meant to or want to live.

All that happens to us in our lives—whether it be good or bad—presents great opportunities for emotional and spiritual growth. You can find greater peace, joy, hope, renewed purpose, and freedom as well as greater opportunities and bigger dreams in the midst of your challenges. The principles and keys to overcoming adversity that I have shared with you in this book will work for you if you consistently and diligently work to apply these principles to your daily life.

The first step to discovering freedom in the midst of your challenges that I discussed in this book, is to always remember that even though you may be experiencing circumstances over which you have no control, you always have the ability to choose your response, attitude, and perception about those circumstances. You are never truly a prisoner of hard circumstances because you are always free to choose your response. Learning to not allow your circumstances to dictate your attitude is one of the most essential keys to overcoming adversity. Remembering that your attitude is a choice is a vital key to living an empowered life.

The second principle of the power of gratitude that I discussed in this book is pivotal in finding freedom. Learning to develop an attitude of gratitude and remembering all of your blessings and assets, even in the midst of painful or challenging circumstances, will have a direct impact on the quality of your life because gratitude shifts your focus away from what is hard or painful to what is right in your life. Remember that many of your blessings are actually hidden treasures or things that you simply take for granted. Learning to truly appreciate the gifts you have been given will be invaluable in your life.

Remembering to speak words that are life-affirming, that bolster and support you, and are lined up according to truth will help you reach the destination in your life that you desire. Remembering the incredible power that your words hold and how they can and do color your experiences, will have a tremendous impact on your life, no matter what you are going through. Old verbal habits may be hard to break, but each time you notice yourself thinking or speaking negatively about your circumstances, you need to see it as something that is robbing you of your freedom as well as your highest potential.

New speaking habits can be created the same way your old habits were created—through practicing them daily. When you change your language to what is positive, you begin expecting positive results rather than negative, which will dramatically change your life.

Learning to discover the opportunities for growth and change in the midst of your pain and challenges is vital to keep you moving into a life of true freedom. Life presents us with many opportunities every day, regardless of what we are going through. When you are going through painful experiences, it can be difficult to understand the potential that lies in your adversities. However, realizing the opportunities to transform your own or someone else's life in the midst of adversity can literally be life-changing as well as cause you to turn your defeat, pain, and hardship into victory. Being able to extract a deeper meaning from your suffering will take you from a place of just surviving into thriving. Finding renewed purpose in the very thing that is your greatest challenge will help heal you, as well as assist you to heal others.

Learning to discover peace of mind, find real hope, and create and allow more joy in your life (which I talked about in the last chapter), regardless of your circumstances, will also bring you to a higher level of healing and living.

I love what John L. Mason says in his book, *Let Go of Whatever Makes You Stop*: "Don't postpone joy. Joy is the most infallible sign of the presence of God. It is the echo of God's life within us." Even in the hardest of circumstances, it is possible to find real joy. I have also always loved this scripture found in Isaiah 26:3: "He will keep in perfect peace all those who trust in him, whose thoughts turn often to the Lord" (Living Bible version).

I believe we can't control the length of our life or many of the circumstances that come into our lives, but we can control the width and depth of our lives by discovering peace of mind, finding hope, and creating more joy in our lives—even when we are experiencing challenging circumstances.

I want to end with this scripture found in Isaiah 43:18–19: "Remember not the former things, neither consider the things of old. Behold I will do a new thing, now it shall spring forth; shall you not know it? I will even make a way in the wilderness, and rivers in the desert." I love this because to me it is the promise of God to make all things beautiful in our lives, regardless of how hard they seem.

It is my greatest hope that you have found some life-changing truths in this book that will take you into a freer way of living, even if you are experiencing hard circumstances. As you come to the end of this book, this is really your beginning into a new way of living. The more you come to understand the transformative power of these five empowering choices, the more you will know true freedom in your life. May your life be fulfilling and richly blessed!

ABOUT SHAUNA

Shauna Bruce-Hamburger is a Motivational Speaker, Life Coach, and owner of "Divine Potential." Shauna was born with spina bifida, but has always believed in living life with a positive attitude despite living with a disability. Shauna has a Bachelor of Science degree in Wellness Management from Black Hills State University and truly has a passion for helping others live healthier and more fulfilling lives.

Shauna is a Wyoming native, but currently lives in Nebraska with her husband, Loren. Shauna has had the experience of writing a monthly newspaper column for three years in the area of health/wellness and personal development for the *News Letter Journal* in Newcastle Wyoming.

Shauna is the founder and owner of Divine Potential, her life coaching and motivational speaking business. Divine Potential is dedicated to helping others maximize their highest potential. Shauna loves inspiring people every day through her business, and feels honored to be able to make a positive difference in the world. So Shauna wanted to share with you what her very rewarding business is all about. Shauna's most requested seminar topics include "Stress-Less and Be More Productive," as well as her "Beyond Adversity and Into Freedom" keynote.

I have always believed that each one of us has untapped, God-given ability and potential. One of my greatest passions in life is helping people find and live in their highest potential. Through coaching with people, I help them discover what is holding them back from living their best life.

"Divine Potential" works with people through life coaching and motivational seminars and to help you find greater fulfillment as well as helping you to live a happier, healthier, richer life. I have always believed that people have more power and greatness inside of them than they realize. It can be so easy to get lost or stuck in our circumstances and end up settling for a life of mediocrity rather than wholeness and true fulfillment. Divine potential can help you discover the greatness inside of you and will challenge you to tap into all that is within you in order to live life at your highest level.

My seminars and life coaching programs cover a gamut of topics that could help free you of whatever is holding you back from living your best lives, from stress management and healthy living to overcoming adversity.

I have always truly loved helping those around me learn to rise above their obstacles to embrace life and live the most fulfilling life possible! It is my greatest desire that through my business I can bring hope, healing, and inspiration to those around me. Because of the issues I have faced in living with spina bifida, and how I have learned to overcome these circumstances, I am a person committed to promoting greater purpose and fulfillment in life by helping people uncover their highest potential through helping them to become free from the limitations that hold them back from the life they desire.

I have faced many of my own challenges in living a life with spina bifida, yet have beat many odds. It is my constant desire to live my life from a place of true joy, passion, and love for life. My family and friends consider me a miracle, and I attribute that to my attitude, my family's faith and support, and my faith in God.

If you are feeling stuck in your life today and you desire to live a richer, more fulfilling life, give me a call and learn how we can work together to create the life you truly desire. If you know someone who would be interested in hosting one of my seminars, please feel free to visit my Web site at www.divinepotential.com or e-mail me at shaunadb@gmail.com or call me at ? ‛hank you and God bless you!

Shauna Bruce-Hamburger

shaunadb@ gmail.com
www.divinepotential.com

"Our chief want is someone who will inspire us to be what we know we could be"

—Ralph Waldo Emerson.

WHAT IS SPINA BIFIDA?

Spina Bifida is the most common permanently disabling birth defect. Spina Bifida is a neural tube defect that happens in the first month of pregnancy when the spinal column doesn't close completely. There are 65 million women at risk of having a baby born with Spina Bifida. Every day, an average of 8 births are affected by Spina Bifida or a similar birth defect of the brain and spine. Each year, about 3,000 pregnancies are affected by these birth defects.

THE CHALLENGES OF SPINA BIFIDA

The effects of Spina Bifida are different for every person. Up to 90 percent of children with the worst form of Spina Bifida have hydrocephalus (fluid on the brain) and must have surgery to insert a "shunt" that helps drain the fluid—the shunt stays in place for the lifetime of the person. Other conditions include full or partial paralysis, bladder and bowel control difficulties, learning disabilities, depression, latex allergy, and social and sexual issues.

THERE ARE THREE TYPES OF SPINA BIFIDA:

Occulta
Often called hidden Spina Bifida, the spinal cord and the nerves are usually normal and there is no opening on the back. In this relatively

harmless form of Spina Bifida, there is a small defect or gap in a few of the small bones (vertebrae) that make up the spine.

There may be no motor or sensory impairments evident at birth. Subtle, progressive neurologic deterioration often becomes evident in later childhood or adulthood.

In many instances, Spina Bifida Occulta is so mild that there is no disturbance of spinal function at all. Occulta can be diagnosed at any age.

Meningocele

The protective coatings (meninges) come through the open part of the spine like a sac that is pushed out. Cerebrospinal fluid is in the sac and there is usually no nerve damage. Individuals may suffer minor disabilities. Additional problems can develop later in life.

Myelomeningocele

This form of Spina Bifida occurs when the meninges (protective covering of the spinal cord) and spinal nerves come through the open part of the spine. This is the most serious type of Spina Bifida, which causes nerve damage and more severe disabilities.

HOW MANY PEOPLE ARE LIVING WITH SPINA BIFIDA?

SBA estimates that more than 166,000 people in the United States are living with this birth defect. However, this figure is conservative and is based on estimates from the SBA Professional Advisory Council. It is anticipated that the number may be higher as there are 54 million people living with disabilities in the United States.

WHAT CAN BE DONE TO PREVENT SPINA BIFIDA?

Studies have shown that if all women who could become pregnant were to take a multivitamin with the B-vitamin folic acid, the risk of neural tube defects could be reduced by up to 70 percent. Folic acid is a water soluble B-vitamin that helps build healthy cells. Because it is water soluble, folic acid does not stay in the body for very long, so women need to take it every day to help reduce the risk of neural tube defects (NTD).

This information was reprinted from the Spina Bifida Association's Web site - www.spinabifidaassociation.org.

My late brother and best friend Shad Ryon Bruce, July 21, 1976–July 28, 2008.

My late brother, Shad Ryon Bruce, who passed away on July 28, 2008, when he was only thirty-two was a wonderful and very wise human being. Shad wanted to be a motivational speaker from the time he was valedictorian of his high school graduating class. Before Shad died, he was working on creating his own motivational audio series to inspire and encourage others to live their best lives. In order to pay tribute to my brother and his amazing work and wisdom, I wanted to bless you as the reader with a CD of some of his very best personal audios.

Shad had a tremendous wealth of wisdom to share with the world and since he never got to share his wisdom, I consider it a great honor to share his best audios here on this CD at the back of the book.

My family played some of my brother's best personal audios at his memorial service and the response we continue to receive of how Shad's wisdom touched and literally transformed people's lives has been truly amazing.

I knew when Shad passed away I wanted to play a part in carrying on what he started, so it is my hope and prayer that you will be inspired and touched by these audios. To carry on my brother's legacy of wisdom is truly a gift to me and I hope you enjoy the audios as much as I have enjoyed being able to share them with you.

I could not have done this project without the help of my amazing friend, Koree Khongphand-Buckman, however, and I would sincerely like to thank Koree for all she did in getting these audios ready to place in the book. You are an amazing gift to me, Koree, and I truly thank you for all that you are and all you have done for this project!

Please fill out this form and send it to the address below.

Your Name	
Address	
City, State, Zip	
Phone Number	

This order is for _____(quanity) books at $19.95 each.
Plus $6.00 each Shipping _____
For a total cost of: _____
~~Nebraska Residents add 7.0%~~

Shauna Bruce-Hamburger

A_____ NE 68301

shaunadb@ gmail.com

www.divinepotential.com